NATO's Adaptation
Challenges and Opportunities

Uwe Hartmann (ed.)

NATO's Adaptation
Challenges and Opportunities

edited by Uwe Hartmann

2017

Carola Hartmann Miles-Verlag

Bibliografische Information der Deutschen Nationalbibliothek
Die Deutsche Nationalbibliothek verzeichnet diese Publikation in der Deutschen Nationalbibliografie; detaillierte bibliografische Daten sind im Internet über www.dnb.de abrufbar.

© 2017 Carola Hartmann Miles-Verlag
www.miles-verlag.jimdo.com
email: miles-verlag@t-online.de

Alle Rechte, insbesondere das Recht der Vervielfältigung und Verbreitung sowie der Übersetzung, vorbehalten. Kein Teil des Werkes darf in irgendeiner Form (durch Fotokopie, Mikrofilm oder ein anderes Verfahren) ohne schriftliche Genehmigung des Verlages reproduziert oder unter Verwendung elektronischer Systeme gespeichert, verarbeitet, vervielfältigt oder verbreitet werden.

Herstellung: BOD – Books on Demand, Norderstedt

ISBN 978-3-945861-59-2

Umschlagbilder: NATO / Jan Ballast

Printed in Germany

Table of Contents

Introduction   7

Lutz Mühlhöfer
NATO's current Relationship Development Efforts in the MENA-Region in the Light of increasing Security Challenges on the Southern Flank   11

Jörg Modey
The North Atlantic, Forgotten Geography of NATO?   23

Willi Bentzinger
Is Russia Still a Technological Power?   45

Jan Ballast
Transatlantic Intelligence Cooperation. Strengthening NATO's First Line of Defense   61

Caroline Linzenmeier
A "Resilient" Strategic Communication – Enhancing the Alliance's Resilience by a strong and coherent Collective Voice   77

Uwe Hartmann
The Evolution of the Hybrid Threat and Resilience as a Countermeasure   93

Frank Wasgindt
Smart Power as a relevant Instrument for a future NATO Strategy   115

About the Authors   128

Introduction
by Uwe Hartmann

Since the 11 September 2001 terror assaults and beyond, NATO has faced significant challenges of political purpose, strategy and the changing face of contemporary conflict. Its involvement in such operations as in Afghanistan has been something other than a true success story. Moreover, the post 2008 campaign of Russia's assertive foreign and security polices laid bare the deficiencies of NATO and its member states in military capabilities, readiness and sustainability on the continent of Europe in the contemporary adaptation of Article V in its more or less original sense. NATO's political and strategic cohesion is challenged by the divergent interests between the Eastern and Southern European countries as they react to the variety of threats arising from irredentism and jihadism. As if these dilemmas were not enough, the citizens in many European states habituated to the joys of what they deem to be perpetual peace seem to be disconnected from what NATO is doing in policy and strategy to adapt to the new security environment.

This volume intends to analyze some of the most pressing challenges of NATO's adaption in its analytical complexity.

Lutz Mühlhöfer and Jörg Modey look at two regions that need intense strategic reflection. These regions are NATO's Southern and the Atlantic theaters. Mühlhöfer argues that NATO should offer added value in order to enhance the cooperation with the states in NATO's southern region. He proposes to invite MENA partners to develop a commonly designed and authored strategic vision with the capacity to produce a truly Combined Crisis Response. The South deserves a tailored engagement of the Alliance that includes the implementation of Cooperative Security Guaranties. Jörg Modey's main proposition is that along with continental strategy, the maritime realm of the Atlantic has been more and more neglected in NATO's strategic documents and planning, while Russia and also China have significantly increased their naval activities recently. Again, the North Atlantic may become a major theatre of operations.

Willi Bentzinger analyses the technological power of Russia so much in the news because of cyber conflict. Specific areas exist where Russia is at least on par with NATO member states. The Russian military modernization programs, particularly the Anti-Access and Area Denial (A2AD) capabilities which have built on forces and weapons with a long heritage, challenge NATO forces. For instance, the latter have stripped their combat echelons of artillery and anti-aircraft defenses to its intense peril and must rediscover old truths which the Russians seem never to have forgotten for a minute. However, the Russian space programs as well as its vulnerabilities in cyber space offer opportunities for cooperation with the Alliance.

Jan Ballast delves into the details of NATO's intelligence. On 21 October 2016, NATO appointed its first Assistant Secretary General for Intelligence and Security (ASG-I&S), a distinguished name: Dr. Arndt Freiherr Freytag von Loringhoven. This paper assesses the future of intelligence sharing within the Alliance following the ASG-I&S' recent creation of a joint intelligence division. Based on theory, practice and insider knowledge, Jan Ballast offers six recommendations to enhance intelligence as NATO's first line of defense made more acute by so called hybrid threats as well as the necessity for crisis mobilization to uphold reassurance and enhanced forward presence.

Caroline Linzenmeier and Uwe Hartmann discuss the new/old concept of resilience from two different angles. Caroline Linzenmeier focuses on Strategic Communication, while Uwe Hartmann analyses strategy-making within the Alliance. Both, Linzenmeier and Hartmann agree that NATO's understanding of resilience should be more comprehensive in perhaps the aspects of real war as laid out by Clausewitz. Linzenmeier thoroughly describes the latest changes in information warfare. She argues that Russia leads the narrative with its assault on western democracy as well as the attempt once again to portray NATO as the aggressor, while NATO as well as its member states show shortfalls in a coherent strategic communication to dispel Russian information warfare, and to promote the member states' and the Alliance's resilience for collective defense. Referring to classical and contemporary strategic thought, Uwe Hartmann reveals the resilience dimensions of NATO's strategy-making and its military adaptation that are indispensable for the utility of force in collective defense and crisis management and, thus, for NATO's future relevance. The Russian way of strategy-making, that is, its concentration in very few hands behind closed doors and its remarkable aggressiveness, poses a significant threat to NATO. Based on a critical analysis of NATO's strategic culture, Uwe Hartmann underlines what needs to be changed rapidly within NATO.

Finally, Frank Wasgindt offers his reflections on hard, soft and smart power and potential consequences for NATO. Generosity, Beauty and Brilliance are the currencies to make NATO more attractive. To achieve these goals, NATO should consider a more active and creative role in providing information to the public and to improve its education and training efforts, including the foundation of NATO universities.

All authors have endeavored to offer not only conclusions of their analyses but also recommendations for action. They share the conviction that civil and military personnel should engage in public discourse to broaden the strategic knowledge on security issues.

Lutz Mühlhöfer
NATO's current Relationship Development Efforts in the MENA-Region in the Light of increasing Security Challenges on the Southern Flank

Introduction

This article contributes to discussing NATO's perspective and evaluating its relationship development in the Middle East and North Africa (MENA).

The prevailing conditions in the MENA Region exceed our worst expectation for the already crisis-torn Southern Flank of the Alliance. First and foremost NATO members in Southern Europe perceive the consequences of civil war, Islamic terrorism and mass migration arising from the MENA Region as a truly destabilizing threat.[1] Moreover the ramifications of the pervasive crisis in the region have a direct effect on European and U.S. societies and their political systems.[2]

During the Warsaw Summit (8-9 July 2016) the Allies sought to define NATO's role in dealing with the complexity of threats emerging from the South. The ongoing discussion within the Alliance about a new strategic concept targeting, inter alia, the Southern Flank are likely to be prioritized[3] since the third strategic pillar Cooperative Security remains underdeveloped[4] and the Mediterranean Dialogue (MD) and the Istanbul Cooperation Initiative (ICI) deem to be reinvigorated.[5]

Cooperative Security is one of NATO's essential core tasks and it reiterates the commitment to develop relations with countries of the

---

[1] Karl-Heinz Kamp *"Why NATO Needs a New Strategic Concept"*, NDC Research Report 09/16 – November 2016, p. 3.

[2] Alexandra De Hoop Scheffer, Martin Michelot, Martin Quencez, *"Southern Challenges and the Regionalization of the Transatlantic Security Partnership"*, The German Marshall Fund of the United States, 2017 / No. 1, p. 1.

[3] Hans Binnendijk, *"NATO's future: A tale of three summits"*, Center for Transatlantic Relations, Johns Hopkins University SAIS, November 2016, p. 2.

[4] Ibid. p. 4.

[5] Ibid. p. 5.

Mediterranean and Gulf Region.[6] The historical evolution of the Mediterranean Dialogue and the Istanbul Cooperation Initiative and NATO's initial objectives in that regard will be used as a point of departure to reassess NATO's 'ends', 'ways' and 'means' devoted to promote security through cooperation on its Southern Flank.

Against the background of the geopolitical upheavals stemming from the MENA Region a simple adjustment of the partnership programs is merely adequate, at this instant NATO is reaching a crossroads to a renewed and more ambitious approach to deeper cooperation.

With the U.S. shifting its strategic focus away from the Middle East leaving room to maneuver for Russia's re-emergence in the region and for other actors to engage in proxy wars, the urgent need for action in terms of developing a strategic vision for the Southern Flank, that includes regional partner outreach, has never been more evident.

NATO's rational for Cooperative Security in the MENA-Region – ends, ways and means

NATO maintains two frameworks to collaborate with MENA countries. The MD, founded in 1994, was predominantly designed as a multilateral platform (now 28 plus 7) offering supplementary bilateral programs since 2006, and intends to foster cooperation with Arab countries such as Mauritania, Morocco, Algeria, Tunisia, Egypt and Jordan as well as with Israel. Consequently the unresolved problems of the Palestine conflict are undermining efforts to find common ground for security strategies with the Arab partners and remain a persistent obstacle for the development of the Dialogue. The ICI, founded in 2004, was essentially designed as a bilateral partnership program (now 28 plus 1). It is mainly geared towards cooperation with the countries of the Arab Peninsular, namely the members of the Gulf Cooperation Council (GCC). This initiative remained short of NATO's ambitions due to the fact that only Kuwait, Bahrain, Qatar and the UAE joined the affiliate program. Saudi Arabia and Oman

---

[6] Strategic Concept for the Defence and Security of the Members of the North Atlantic Treaty Organization, Summit in Lisbon, 19-20 November 2010, p.32. http://www.nato.int/nato_static_fl2014/assets/pdf/pdf_publications/20120214_strategic-concept-2010-eng.pdf

favor a cautious approach to NATO and refrain from joining the initiative for different reasons: As the regional hegemon Saudi Arabia doesn't appreciate being approached on the same framework level as its GCC partners and Oman tries to avoid irritating Tehran caused by a rapprochement to the Western Alliance.[7] The absence of Saudi Arabia as the regional power within the ICI remains a persistent shortfall for NATO's outreach to the region.[8]

Ends: For more than 20 years, NATO has had the ambition to transfer stability beyond the alliance's borders and to foster Defense Capacity Building among Mediterranean and Middle East partners as a means to create "strategic depth" on its Southern Flank.[9] These initiatives were intended to improve NATO's situational awareness and regional understanding of the MENA security environment.

Ways: Unlike NATO's outreach to eastern European countries over the past 25 years the regional networks MD and ICI were never designed to initiate accession talks aiming at a full NATO membership.[10] In fact the overarching objective for these partnership programs was high-level public diplomacy approaching the region's elites and officials.[11] On tactical and operational levels the cooperation activities extend from interoperability exercises and maritime security over intelligence sharing to counter-terrorist cooperation and the fight against the proliferation of weapons of mass destruction.[12] On a working level NATO opens the doors of the NATO School in Ober-

---

[7] Jean Loup Samaan, *"The Strategic Significance of the New NATO-ICI Regional Centre in Kuwait"*, NATO Defense College Foundation, p. 1.

[8] Jean-Loup Samaan, *"NATO's Middle East Partnership Policy after the Warsaw Summit: Time for a Realistic Agenda?"* The German Marshall Fund of the United States, 2017 / No.1, p. 4.

[9] Presentation by M.Gen D'Addario, Deputy Chief Ops, ITA MoD during Field Study 1, Rome, 20.03.2017

[10] Istanbul Cooperation Initiative, official text, paragraph 3,e, last updated 23.11.2009. http://www.nato.int/cps/en/natolive/official_texts_21017.htm

[11] Tommy Steiner, *"NATO and its Middle East and Mediterranean Partners: Taking NATO's Role in its Southern Flank to a New Strategic Level"*, The German Marshall Fund of the United States, 2017 / No. 1, p. 8.

[12] Pierre Razoux, *"What future for NATO's Istanbul Cooperation Initiative?"*, NATO Defense College Research Paper No.55 – January 2010, p. 2.

ammergau and the NATO Defense College in Rome and offers a wide range of education and training programs and access to the Partnership Realtime Information, Management and Exchange System (e-Prime).[13]

Means: Even though NATO never assumed a strategic role in the Mediterranean and the Middle East it proved its ability to go beyond soft power engagement during the 2011 operation in Libya involving four regional partners, UAE, Qatar, Jordan and Morocco. In a results-orientated approach one could argue that the partnership went through its baptism of fire demonstrating not only the will but also the capability to engage in a crisis management scenario in a combined way." At the end of the day, the operation in Libya demonstrated that NATO can operate in the region irrespective of pre-existing negative perceptions."[14] And all this was achieved within seven months without a single coalition loss of life.

NATO's Operation Sea Guardian that was launched after the Warsaw Summit in 2016 is another example of an active engagement of the Alliance that has a lot of gross potential in terms of partnership inclusion.[15]

Is NATO's outreach to the MENA Region on track – Are we doing the right things and are we doing the things right?

The institutional framework of MD and ICI haven't changed much since their foundation[16], which doesn't imply that nothing has been achieved. NATO is observing an increasing interest of some MD and

---

[13] Pierre Razoux, *"What future for NATO's Istanbul Cooperation Initiative?"*, NATO Defense College Research Paper No.55 – January 2010, p. 3.

[14] Tommy Steiner, *"NATO and its Middle East and Mediterranean Partners: Taking NATO's Role in its Southern Flank to a New Strategic Level"*, The German Marshall Fund of the United States, 2017 / No. 1, p. 9.

[15] NATO Homepage, *Operation Sea Guardian*, http://www.nato.int/cps/en/natohq/topics_136233.htm?selectedLocale=en

[16] Jean-Loup Samaan, *"NATO's Middle East Partnership Policy after the Warsaw Summit: Time for a Realistic Agenda?"* The German Marshall Fund of the United States, 2017 / No. 1, p. 3.

ICI partners on an institutional level. Israel, Bahrain and Kuwait are intending to open a permanent mission at NATO Headquarters whilst Jordan will accredit an official mission to NATO that is run by its embassy to Belgium. In a reciprocal approach NATO Secretary-General Jens Stoltenberg has inaugurated the NATO-ICI Regional Centre in Kuwait in January 2017 as a gateway to the whole Arab Peninsula. This institutional footing in the Middle East constitutes an unprecedented milestone in the history of the ICI and could provide new momentum.[17] It is noteworthy to mention that this endeavor was initiated by the Ruler of the Emirate of Kuwait and not by NATO![18] At first glance this seems surprising, but some Gulf Cooperation Council (GCC) members have realized that new Iranian-US/European relations could emerge at the expense of GCC countries.[19] Hence, invigorating the ties within the ICI could help to impede this scenario.

These recent developments and the numerous activities on political, diplomatic, institutional, operational and working levels over the past two decades have shown that "NATO's co-operative security can offer useful tools in a meaningful way to the entire region."[20] The establishment of a partnership outside the Western world is undoubtedly a troublesome endeavor. We should keep in mind that all this was achieved despite the cultural based reluctance of Arab rulers to cooperate with institutions. Generally speaking the Arab leadership

---

[17] Jean Loup Samaan, *"The Strategic Significance of the New NATO-ICI Regional Centre in Kuwait"*, NATO Defense College Foundation, p. 1.
http://www.natofoundation.org/02/the-strategic-significance-of-the-new-nato-ici-regional-centre-in-kuwait/

[18] Jean Loup Samaan, *"The Strategic Significance of the New NATO-ICI Regional Centre in Kuwait"*, NATO Defense College Foundation, p.2.

[19] Ebtesam AL-Ketbi, *"The Gulf needs a real Istanbul Cooperation Initiative Plus"*, Arab Geopolitics In Turmoil, Perceptions, Unknowns and Policies, Conference Organized by the NATO Defense College Foundation, Rome 25.-26.02.2016, p. 78.
http://www.natofoundation.org/wp-content/uploads/2016/07/NDCF-Arab-Geopolitics-Feb-2016.pdf

[20] Arab Geopolitics In Turmoil, Perceptions, Unknowns and Policies, Conference Organized by the NATO Defense College Foundation, Rome 25.-26.02.2016, p. 1.
http://www.natofoundation.org/wp-content/uploads/2016/07/NDCF-Arab-Geopolitics-Feb-2016.pdf

has a strong preference to cooperate with affiliates who they are personally acquainted with.[21]

The instability within the MENA Region is mainly caused by socioeconomical deficiencies and not by dysfunctional militaries within the region. Hence NATO can't solve the core problem which ultimately leads to a long-term coping strategy in which NATO can contribute by assisting partners in establishing a secure environment. Keeping this in mind, it appears that NATO is doing the right things with its capacity building outreach to the MENA Region. The counterfactual approach would also teach us that without a MD or ICI we would probably identify the need to implement such a cooperation network. The existing strategic concept of the Alliance with its core tasks of Crisis Management and Cooperative Security provides a feasible foundation to assist in stabilizing the South. But is this really the sustainable regional architecture based on cooperative security that we desperately need? Is NATO doing the things right or is there still room for improvement?

NATO doesn't call its outreach programs to the region 'partnership' for any specific reason – it has none! NATO appeared timid in its approach to MENA partners by ruling out membership negotiations from the beginning and limiting its partnership offers to Dialogues and Initiatives. Even though the outreach approaches the region's elites and leaders it remains a lower scale collaboration. Against the background of existing challenges evolving from the MENA region this simply doesn't suffice. NATO needs to define a new spectrum of collaboration with the region that goes beyond convening in conferences in the framework of public diplomacy. Cooperative Security is not tailored for the partners in the South since its needs to address countries like Austria and Finland as well. But the Alliance has never developed a clear strategic vision for its regional engagement in the South within its existing strategic concept. Hence the reluctance of the regional partners to increase their level of ambition in the 'partnership' can't be surprising in light of NATO's unclear concept for the South. What needs to be done? First of all the Allies need to find

---

[21] This reflects the authors personal experience as the German Defence Attache´ accredited to the UAE, Kuwait and Qatar from 2009-2012

consensus on a strategic vision for the South. Unlike the Eastern Flank there is no clear identified aggressor that mainly challenges NATO's Collective Defence capability. A strategic vision for the South should tackle threats emerging from the South without targeting the state actors of the region. On the contrary, NATO needs to collaborate closely with these state actors in the fight against non-state actors like transnational terrorism, decentralized militia groups, organized immigration crime and other illegal trafficking.[22] The Alliance should lift the partnership programs to the next level and develop a new strategic vision for the South by including its regional partners' right from the definition phase. Advocating an active integrated Arab contribution should not be condemned: "Real joint authorship between NATO and its regional partners would undoubtedly enhance the perceived relevance of NATO in the Region".[23]

NATO is a western alliance that commits itself to defend western values. This fundamental mindset could potentially lead to misunderstanding with the leadership of the MENA region. In its Public Diplomacy approach to the elites of the Arab World NATO should avoid a value-based discussion and concentrate on identifying a set of common interests. In the interaction with the Arab leadership the distinction between 'values' and 'interest' is far more than semantic nitpicking.[24] Taking this into account a reassessment of common ground with partners would be more promising.

What are we prepared to offer, how do we create incentives for our partners to deepen the cooperation? The inauguration of the NATO-ICI Regional Centre in Kuwait is an adequate measure and a step in the right direction. Increasing NATO's visible footprint in the region would demonstrate NATO's will to go beyond its timid mode and

---

[22] Ebtesam AL-Ketbi, *"The Gulf needs a real Istanbul Cooperation Initiative Plus"*, Arab Geopolitics In Turmoil, Perceptions, Unknowns and Policies, Conference Organized by the NATO Defense College Foundation, Rome 25.-26.02.2016, p. 77.

[23] Tommy Steiner, *"NATO and its Middle East and Mediterranean Partners: Taking NATO's Role in its Southern Flank to a New Strategic Level"*, The German Marshall Fund of the United States, 2017 / No. 1, p. 12.

[24] This is the author's personal conclusion after attending the International Conference on "NATO-UAE Relations and the Way Forward in the Istanbul Cooperation Initiative" in Abu Dhabi, UAE 29.-30.10.2009

show commitment to the destiny of the region. To be more attractive for its partners NATO needs to develop Cooperative Security *Guaranties* by establishing contingency plans for possible NATO interventions that are jointly authored together with partner nations. Based on the common understanding that accession talks with NATO's partners in the South are not desired, NATO could nevertheless, in the case of a commonly identified crisis, consider assisting with guarantied Intelligence exchange, logistical support or the secondment of NATO advisers upon request of a partner. Changing from a mere 'transfer of stability' towards a more dynamic 'projecting of stability' would give NATO's relationship development in the MENA region a fresh impetus.

In order to overcome the described obstacles within the partnership programs, NATO needs to invent a new partnership system by combining the advantages of the bi- and multi-lateral *approach in a cluster-orientated dialogue*. Developing a cooperation spreadsheet with cooperation action items organized in matrix rows and the individual partner nations organized in matrix columns could offer an individualized and tailored cooperation scheme. The advantages of the multi-lateral approach could be useful in areas where individual partner nation's interests overlap, regardless of their geographical location. Undoubtedly this technocratic approach needs to be supported by a diplomatic illustration campaign.

This flexible approach would circumnavigate obstacles within the existing MD and ICI outreach and offer a cooperation framework that is also adjustable in terms of partnership commitment. The highest level of commitment for NATO would be the offer of Cooperative Security Guaranties.

Conclusion

NATO members seem to be highly reluctant to conduct their second core task of Crisis Management with 'boots on the ground' in the MENA Region and the idea that NATO commands while MENA partners conduct the beastly job remains an illusion.[25] If this fundamental attitude within the Alliance prevails then the third strategic pillar of Cooperative Security consequentially has to gain relevance. Otherwise, regional competitors like Russia will dominate the cooperative domain in NATO's southern sphere of interest. NATO needs to strive for a true strategic role and offer added value by inviting MENA partners to develop a commonly designed and authored strategic vision with the capacity to produce a truly Combined Crisis Response. The South deserves a tailored engagement of the Alliance. Implementing Cooperative Security *Guaranties* as NATO's sign of an unequivocal commitment to the region's destiny and a flexible framework using the *Matrix-Approach* could help to increase NATO's relevance as a security provider for the region. Complementing this new approach by a public diplomacy campaign that respects the cultural particularities of Arab leaders could reinvigorate NATO's outreach to the MENA Region dramatically.

Whatever the Alliance decides to do – it needs to take action soon and find the right balance between Quick Wins and Long Term Gains. As well as the deficiencies within the existing partnership programs and the imponderables connected with the security challenges that are emerging from the Southern Flank, NATO is additionally confronted with the receding ambitions of the U.S. to engage militarily in the region. Taking the reemergence of Russia in the Middle East into the equation the urgency becomes even more evident. In fact Russia appears as a competitor in the Cooperative Security Domain in the region. If the alliance doesn't build capacity then Russia will!

---

[25] Alexandra De Hoop Scheffer, Martin Michelot, Martin Quencez, *"Southern Challenges and the Regionalization of the Transatlantic Security Partnership"*, The German Marshall Fund of the United States, 2017 / No. 1, p. 2.

Bibliography

AL-Ketbi, Ebtesam, *"The Gulf needs a real Istanbul Cooperation Initiative Plus"*, Arab Geopolitics in Turmoil, Perceptions, Unknowns and Policies, Conference Organized by the NATO Defense College Foundation, Rome 25.-26.02.2016, p. 78.
http://www.natofoundation.org/wp-content/uploads/2016/07/NDCF-Arab-Geopolitics-Feb-2016.pdf

Arab Geopolitics in Turmoil, Perceptions, Unknowns and Policies, Conference Organized by the NATO Defense College Foundation, Rome 25.-26.02.2016
http://www.natofoundation.org/wp-content/uploads/2016/07/NDCF-Arab-Geopolitics-Feb-2016.pdf

Binnendijk, Hans, *"NATO's future: A tale of three summits"*, Center for Transatlantic Relations, Johns Hopkins University SAIS, November 2016

De Hoop Scheffer Alexandra, Michelot Martin, Quencez Martin, *"Southern Challenges and the Regionalization of the Transatlantic Security Partnership"*, The German Marshall Fund of the United States, 2017 / No. 1

Kamp, Karl-Heinz, *"Why NATO Needs a New Strategic Concept"*, NDC Research Report 09/16 – November 2016

NATO, Strategic Concept for the Defence and Security of the Members of the NATO, Summit in Lisbon, 19-20 November 2010
http://www.nato.int/nato_static_fl2014/assets/pdf/pdf_publications/20120214_strategic-concept-2010-eng.pdf

Razoux, Pierre, *"What future for NATO's Istanbul Cooperation Initiative?"*, NATO Defense College Research Paper No.55 – January 2010

Razoux, Pierre, Seminar Report, *"NATO and Gulf Security"*, NATO Defense College Rome, 02.-03.12.2009

Samaan, Jean-Loup, *"NATO's Middle East Partnership Policy after the Warsaw Summit: Time for a Realistic Agenda?"*, The German Marshall Fund of the United States, 2017 / No. 1

Samaan, Jean-Loup, *"The Strategic Significance of the New NATO-ICI Regional Centre in Kuwait"*, NATO Defense College Foundation, http://www.natofoundation.org/02/the-strategic-significance-of-the-new-nato-ici-regional-centre-in-kuwait/

Sobecki, Nicholas Kirk, *"Why NATO Should Cooperate with Fellow Regional Organizations"*, Atlantic-Community.Org, 21.06.2016 http://www.atlantic-community.org/print/-/asset_publisher/Bwkm77BDDnXu/content/why-nato-should-cooperate-with-fellow-regional-organizations

Steiner, Tommy, *"NATO and its Middle East and Mediterranean Partners: Taking NATO's Role in its Southern Flank to a New Strategic Level"*, The German Marshall Fund of the United States, 2017 / No. 1

Wehrey, Frederic, *"Transatlantic Security Assistance in Fractured States: The Troubling Case of Libya"*, The German Marshall Fund of the United States, 2017 / No. 1

Jörg Modey
The North Atlantic, Forgotten Geography of NATO?

> *"You may be amazed how many ideas you get in terms of relationships or dangers, if you look at the map from the standpoint of your own interests and then of the others."*[1]

Introduction

Two years away from NATO's 70th anniversary it seems appropriate to consider whether the notion of 'Atlanticism' still makes sense, politically and militarily. In this context, it is worth noting that the Washington Treaty of 1949 is based on values <u>and</u> geography.

The geographical linkage between the North Atlantic Ocean and the creation of the defense treaty is not a coincidence; it has been the pivot of collective defense and a *critical requirement* throughout the existence of the Alliance up until the end of the Cold War.

The twelve original signatories of the Treaty agreed on the 4th April 1949 in Washington D.C. "[…] to promote stability and well-being in the **North Atlantic Area**."[2] Ten signatories actually have a coastline on the North Atlantic Ocean. The first strategic concept of December 1949 describes the "North Atlantic family of nations."[3] Six strategic concepts later, no reminiscence to the ocean which gave the Alliance its name is left in the conceptual documentaries.[4]

---

[1] Brezinski, Zbigniew, "On the World: On global politics", *Center for Strategic International Studies, Interview*, (06. October 2015), accessed 10 April 2017
https://www.youtube.com/watch?v=7HDBbPzbONM

[2] Preamble to the North Atlantic Treaty (1949), *NATO*, Accessed 10 April 2017
http://www.nato.int/cps/en/natohq/official_texts_17120.htm

[3] The strategic concept for the defence of the North Atlantic Area, D.C. 6/1, (01 December 1949), *NATO*, para III 6. (a), Accessed 06 April 2017
http://www.nato.int/docu/stratdoc/eng/a491201a.pdf

[4] "Active Engagement, Modern Defence", Strategic Concept for the Defence and Security of the Members of the North Atlantic Treaty Organisation adopted by Heads of State and Government in Lisbon, 19 November 2010.

This paper will define the geography, compare the strategic heritages of NATO and mainly Russia and identify the strategic challenges of today. In doing so, the paper intends to verify that: The North Atlantic Ocean is as vital to the Alliance as ever and remains the (military) centre of gravity for NATO's collective defence.

Defining the Geography

Article 6 of the Treaty limits the Parties of the area to the North Atlantic Area north of the Tropic of Cancer.[5] The subsequent strategic concept of 1952, *Massive Retaliation*, defined the geographical areas of the Alliance in more depth; they remained unaltered until the end of the Cold War: "This setting comprises Continental Europe (consisting of Western Europe, flanked by Scandinavia and Southern Europe), the British Isles and North America. The defence of these also involves their contiguous sea areas, and in particular the North Atlantic, the English Channel and North Sea, and the Mediterranean."[6]

In theory, the northern end of this geography could be the North Pole. However, the strategic implications of this region with respect to geopolitics[7] and the military[8] are distinct and require consideration as a separate *theatre of operation*. For the purpose of this paper the geographical limit of the North Atlantic northbound will include the Scandinavian and Kola Peninsulas, Iceland and the adjacent Greenland and Canada <u>without</u> the Arctic (Ocean).

---

[5] Article 6 (1) North Atlantic Treaty (1949) , *NATO*, Accessed 06 April 2017
http://www.nato.int/cps/en/natohq/official_texts_17120.htm

[6] North Atlantic Military Committee Decision on M.C. 14/1, 9 December 1952, *NATO*, para 18. Accessed 06 April 2017
http://www.nato.int/docu/stratdoc/eng/a521209a.pdf

[7] e.g. "Russian explorers have planted their country's flag on the seabed 4,200m (14,000ft) below the North Pole to further Moscow's claims to the Arctic." *BBC News*, Accessed 19 March 2017.
http://news.bbc.co.uk/2/hi/europe/6927395.stm

[8] Sven G. Holtsmark, "Towards cooperation or confrontation? Security in the High North", *Research Paper No. 45, Research Division, NATO Defense College*, Rome, February 2009

Political and military strategy of the Alliance with respect to the North Atlantic

In 1979 at the height of the Cold War, the following observation was made: "Over the past decade, more than one Northern European Commander has wondered aloud if NATO's leaders were not so distracted by their concentration on the problems of the Central Front that they missed seeing the problems on their northern flank."[9]

This statement could easily apply in 2017. The term *Northern Flank* was commonly used during the bipolar period of the Cold War. If this occurred with reference to the Prussian general and military theorist Clausewitz who defined a flank as "every position which is to be held, even if the enemy passes by it. [...] Therefore, necessarily, all strong positions are flank positions as well"[10], or with a geographic reference to a lateral side[11] as in NATO's 1952 strategic concept[12] is less important. The relevance of the North Atlantic with its Northern Flank between Scandinavia, the North and Baltic Sea, the UK, Iceland and Greenland remained essential.

The military and strategic importance of the North Atlantic was underlined in M.C. 14/1: "The North Atlantic Ocean is the medium whereby the great potential of the Americas can be transported and brought to bear against the enemy in Europe. The security of sea routes within this ocean is a vital requirement."[13] It was asserted that the North Atlantic and the Northern Flank were of such strategic importance, that a war in Europe could not be sustained if the sea

---

[9] Jeffrey G. Barlow, "NATO's Northern Flank: The growing Soviet threat", (01 May 1979), *The Heritage Foundation 15*, Accessed 19 March 2017
http://www.heritage.org/defense/report/natos-northern-flank-the-growing-soviet-threat

[10] Carl von Clausewitz, *On War* (Berlin 1832), Book 6, Chapter 14, Accessed 19 March 2017
https://www.clausewitz.com/readings/OnWar1873/BK6ch14.html

[11] *Collins Concise English Dictionary* (Glasgow 1992)

[12] North Atlantic Military Committee Decision on M.C. 14/1, 9 December 1952, *NATO*, Para 18

[13] Ibid, Para 57.
http://www.nato.int/docu/stratdoc/eng/a521209a.pdf

lines of communication (SLOCs) were interrupted.[14] This has not changed to date! With its own Command & Control (C2) structure the Supreme Allied Commander Atlantic (SACLANT) was to provide for the security of the North Atlantic Area by guarding the SLOCs and denying their use to an enemy.[15]

Literature does not hold a clear definition of a Centre of Gravity (CoG). Clausewitz used the German term *Schwerpunkt* (= Centre of Gravity) without a consistent meaning.[16] NATO defines[17] CoG as *Characteristics, capabilities or localities from which a nation, an alliance, a military force or other grouping derives its freedom of action, physical strength or will to fight*. SHAPE's Comprehensive Operations Planning Directive (COPD)[18] uses a CoG Analysis Matrix which unravels the CoG into *critical capabilities, critical requirements and critical vulnerabilities*. On the political level, NATO's CoG remains most likely the cohesion of the Alliance. On the military level, however the Atlantic Ocean as a geographic theatre of operation is at least a critical requirement of the Alliance and certainly a critical vulnerability to be protected. This vulnerability is certainly not limited to military objectives but also applies to trade transit routes such as oil and gas.

Overall, it can be considered as a military CoG from which the Alliance derives its freedom of action.

The last and current Strategic Concept of NATO: "Active Engagement, Modern Defence" dates from 2010. Within the midst of a transforming process the only remnant to the aforementioned CoG

---

[14] Michael K. Mahon, "Defending Norway and the Northern Flank: Analysis of NATO's Strategic Options", *Naval Postgraduate School* (Monterey 1985),10

[15] NATO Handbook, (29 October 2002), Accessed 19 March 2017
https://web.archive.org/web/20080813225955/http://www.nato.int/docu/handbook/2001/hb120704.htm
SACLANT was active from 20 January 1952 until 19 June 2003 when it was 'transformed' into the Allied Command for Transformation ACT and the remaining tasks were transferred to SACEUR.

[16] Joseph L. Strange and Richard Iron, "Center of Gravity; What Clausewitz Really Meant", *Joint Force Quarterly 35*, NDU, (October 2004), 20 – 27.

[17] NATO Glossary of Terms and Definition, AAP-06 Edition 2014,

[18] Allied Command Operations, Comprehensive Operations Planning Directive Interim V2.0 , 4 October 2013, Figure 4.11

is: "The transatlantic link remains as strong and as important to the preservation of Euro-Atlantic peace and security, as ever."[19] This rather casual remark about upholding the transatlantic link refers more to the political cohesion of the Alliance than to the vital SLOCs. Even NATO's Wales Summit of September 2014, in the aftermath of Russia's unlawful annexation of the Crimea, did not make much reference to the transatlantic area.[20] A first change in perception comes with an initiative by the Ministers of Defense from Norway, France, Iceland and the UK in early 2016 stating that "it is of vital importance that NATO safeguard the sea lines of communication during a crisis or conflict" and further, "Safeguarding NATO's freedom of movement and operation across the North Atlantic is of importance to all of Europe, not only the northern parts of the Alliance."[21] This initiative probably let to the Warsaw Summit Declaration making a clear reference to the North Atlantic, "Taken together, the measures we are approving at this Summit will enhance the security of all Allies and ensure protection of Alliance territory, populations, airspace and sea lines of communication, including across the Atlantic, against all threats from wherever they arise."[22] Is this the beginning of a re-focus towards the vast area of saltwater that gave the Alliance its name?

---

[19] "Active Engagement, Modern Defence".

[20] "Wales Summit Declaration", Issued by the Heads of State and Government participating in the meeting of the North Atlantic Council in Wales, 05 September 2014, Accessed 19 March 2017,
http://www.nato.int/cps/en/natohq/official_texts_112964.htm?mode=pressrelease

[21] Ine Erikson Søreide, „NATO and the North Atlantic, Revitalizing Collective Defense and the Maritime Domain", *PRISM 6*, No.2, Center for Complex Operations (CCO) at the National Defense University (3 August 2016), p. 51.

[22] "Warsaw Summit Communiqué", Issued by the Heads of State and Government participating in the meeting of the North Atlantic Council (Warsaw 9 July 2016), Accessed 19 March 2017, para 23, 38.
http://www.nato.int/cps/en/natohq/official_texts_133169.htm

Standpoints of other actors
a. The Russian Federation

Russian geopolitics and military strategy of the 21st century are largely influenced if not dominated by one man: Vladimir Putin. As the Russian Federation's Prime Minister and presidential candidate[23], Vladimir Putin gave a BBC interview on 05 March 2000 outlining his geopolitical perception: "My position is that our country should be a strong, powerful state [...] Russia is part of the European culture. And I cannot imagine my own country in isolation from Europe and what we often call the civilized world." Under the premises of being accepted as an equal partner, he even goes so far as to not rule out a NATO membership of the Russian Federation in the future.[24] Mainly due to NATO's enlargement policy the theoretical partnership '*at par*', as laid out in the NATO-Russia Founding Act and later in the agreement on the NATO-Russia Council (NRC)[25] was not perceived as such by Russia. Moreover, in the conflict with Georgia in 2008, the Russian Federation considered that it was pursuing the "NATO model", intervening in a sovereign state with military force without a UN Security Council Mandate as NATO did in OPERATION ALLIED FORCE in the Balkans in 1999.[26]

As early as 2001, President Putin approved the new Maritime Doctrine of the Russian Federation which outlines very clearly his perception: "Historically, Russia [is] the leading maritime power, on the basis of its spatial and geophysical features, place and role in global and

---

[23] His first presidential election was on 26 March 200 with a 52,9 % win.

[24] David Frost, "BBC Interview with Frost: Vladimir Putin" (5 March 2000), accessed 20 March 2017,
http://news.bbc.co.uk/hi/english/static/audio_video/programmes/breakfast_with_frost/transcripts/putin5.mar.txt

[25] "Founding Act on Mutual Relations, Cooperation and Security between NATO and the Russian Federation", (Paris, 27 May 1997) Accesses 24 April 2017.
http://www.nato.int/cps/en/natohq/official_texts_25468.htm and
"NATO-Russia Council Joint Statement", (Lisbon, 20 November 2010), Accessed 24 April 2017 http://www.nato.int/cps/en/natohq/news_68871.htm

[26] Keir Giles, "The Military Doctrine of the Russian Federation 2010", *Research Review, NATO Defense College* (Rome February 2010), p. 4.

regional international relations."²⁷ The 2001 Maritime Doctrine even underlines the demand for free access to the Atlantic and for seeking favourable conditions for the Northern Fleet in the North Atlantic.²⁸ Even though it remained largely unnoticed, this early Naval Doctrine was a "systemic document that underlines the national maritime policy and constitutes an integral part of the Russian leadership's strategic planning."²⁹

Fourteen years later and just one month prior to military engagement in Syria, Russia adopted an updated Naval Doctrine. "The revised Naval Doctrine primarily focuses on two regional geostrategic areas: the Atlantic and the Arctic. A process of retrofitting of the Navy began to unfold, and the activities of the Russian Navy in the oceans increased sharply."³⁰

b. China

"No, Greenland does not belong to China"³¹, this headline of an opinion article in the New York Times might raise the question, China in the North Atlantic? And yet, state-linked Chinese companies are increasingly interested in investments and properties in the self-ruled state of Greenland, an autonomous constituent country within the Kingdom of Denmark. Chinese companies such as General Nice Group and Shenghe Resources have been investing in Greenland

---

[27] Maritime Doctrine of the Russian Federation 2020, Approved by President Vladimir Putin (27 July 2001), 2. Regional trends of national maritime policy, Accessed 20 March 2017,
http://www.oceanlaw.org/downloads/arctic/Russian_Maritime_Policy_2020.pdf

[28] Ibid.
http://www.oceanlaw.org/downloads/arctic/Russian_Maritime_Policy_2020.pdf

[29] Ruslan Pukov, "Russia's Naval Doctrine: New Priorities and Benchmarks" *Valdai Club*, (17 August 2015),
http://valdaiclub.com/a/highlights/russia_s_naval_doctrine_new_priorities_and_b enchmarks/

[30] Ibid.

[31] Martin Breum, "No , Greenland Does Not Belong to China", *The New York Times, The Opinion Page*, (20 February 2013), Accessed 01 April 2017,
http://www.nytimes.com/2013/02/21/opinion/no-greenland-does-not-belong-to-china.html

mining companies for some time.[32] It could be an expression of a pure globalised economic approach to scarce resources such as iron ore, uranium and rare earths or a long-term geostrategic approach. Either way, it is most likely that the Chinese state is playing an important role behind the investments abroad.[33] The Danish Prime Minister Lars Løkke Rasmussen has allegedly personally intervened to prevent the General Nice Group from acquiring the old, disused military station Grønnedal.[34] The derelict naval base was only abandoned by the Danish Navy in 2014 and for sale when the Chinese bid to buy it in 2016 possibly caused the reversal of the Danish decision to sell Grønnedal.[35] Danish authorities might worry that Chinese companies will grow so economically significant in Greenland that they can manipulate the smaller and financially weaker Greenland self-rule authorities.[36] It is a fact that, with China's involvement in Greenland, there is yet another powerful player in the geostrategic game over the North Atlantic.

China's activities in Greenland seem to remain unnoticed by NATO.

Reality Check

Whilst NATO's strategic concept focuses on partnerships, Russia very clearly speaks of a perceived military threat created by the enlargement of NATO.[37] The Russian Federation sees the North Atlan-

---

[32] Martin Breum, "Analysis: Did the Danish PM prevent a Chinese acquisition on Greenland", *High North News*, (20 December 2016), Accessed 01 April 2017, http://www.highnorthnews.com/analysis-did-the-danish-pm-prevent-a-chinese-acquisition-on-greenland/

[33] Jichang Lulu, "China, Greenland and competition fort he Arctic", *China Policy Institute: Analysis*, (02 January 2017), Accessed 01 April 2017, https://cpianalysis.org/2017/01/02/china-greenland-and-competition-for-the-arctic/

[34] Breum, *Analysis*

[35] Ibid.

[36] Ibid.

[37] The Military Doctrine of the Russian Federation, Approved by Russian Federation presidential edict (5 February 2010), II 8. The main external military dangers, Accessed 20 March 2017, http://carnegieendowment.org/files/2010russia_military_doctrine.pdf

tic as a strategic geography of its own.

Apart from a purely military perspective, the North Atlantic is a major global commons; sea- and airlines of communication are of strategic importance for North America and Europe and the entire world alike. As in the period of the Cold War, any major operation in Europe or on its periphery could not be initiated or sustained for long without the military capacity from the western side of the Atlantic.[38] This founding paradigm of NATO has not changed in almost 70 years.

Russia's aggressive military posture on the Northern Flank is not yet perceived by NATO as a tangible risk. According to the Danish Defence Intelligence Service (DDIS), a simulated nuclear attack of Russian aircraft with live missiles flying at low altitude towards the Danish island of Bornholm in June 2013 was not seen as a direct military threat to Danish territory.[39] During another exercise named *Arctic, Western MD*, Russian forces in March 2015 simulated an invasion of the four Scandinavian states.[40] Even if it was not seen as a purely military provocation to NATO, the repeated presence of Russian intruders into national airspace with switched-off transponders has led to a series of near mid-air-collisions with civilian airliners.[41]

---

[38] John Barry, "Lessons of Libya for future western military forays", *European Affairs, The European Institute*, (August 2011), Accessed 24 April 2017,
https://www.europeaninstitute.org/index.php/130-european-affairs/ea-august-2011/1417-lessons-of-libya-for-future-western-military-forays

[39] "Russia simulated an attack on Denmark", *The Local dk*, (31 October 2014), Accessed 01 April 2017,
https://www.thelocal.dk/20141031/russia-simulated-a-military-attack-on-denmark

[40] David Blair, "Russian forces practised invasion of Norway, Finland, Denmark and Sweden", *The Telegraph*, (26 June 2015), Accessed 01 April 2017,
http://www.telegraph.co.uk/news/worldnews/europe/russia/11702328/Russian-forces-practised-invasion-of-Norway-Finland-Denmark-and-Sweden.html

[41] "NATO Tracks large-Scale Russian Air Activity in Europe", *SHAPE*, (20 October 2014), Accessed 01 April 2017, http://www.shape.nato.int/nato-tracks-largescale-russian-air-activity-in-europe, See also:
Blair, "Russian forces practised invasion of Norway, Finland, Denmark and Sweden", See also:
In March 2014, a Boeing 737 from Scandinavian Airlines narrowly avoided a mid-air collision with a Russian IL-20 reconnaissance aircraft during a flight from Copenhagen to Rome.

The geopolitical and military ambitions of the Russian Federation outlined in their strategic and doctrinal documents hold up to reality in blue water operations[42] and compared to NATO, they have a clear objective with real capability enhancements. The reopening of military bases on the Kola Peninsula[43]; the reorganization of the command and force structure of the Northern Fleet; the delivery of up to 100 new naval ships by 2020[44]; new anti-access/area-denial (A2/AD)[45] bastions in the Kaliningrad Oblast with anti-ship[46] and ballistic missiles[47]; new and very sophisticated submarines[48] and last but not least the amount, scale and nature of exercise activities[49] of Russian military forces, sends a clear message. On the other hand, NATO and its

---

[42] Elizabeth Zolotukhina, "Can Russia Implement ist New Naval Doctrine", *Centre for Geopolitics & Security in Realism Studies*, (London, 03 August 2015), p. 5

[43] Trude Pettersen, "Plans to reopen military base on Kola Peninsula", *Barents Observer*, (21 February 2014), Accessed 01 April 2014,
http://barentsobserver.com/en/security/2014/02/plans-reopen-military-base-kola-peninsula-21-02

[44] Elizabeth Zolotukhina, "Can Russia Implement its New Naval Doctrine", *Centre for Geopolitics & Security in Realism Studies*, London, (03 August 2015), p. 2.

[45] An appealing definition can be found at Stephan Frühling and Guillaume Lasconjarias, "NATO, A2/AD and the Kaliningrad Challenge", *Survival Vol 58 No 2*, (May 2016), p. 97:
The basic idea of anti-access and area denial is very simple: the best way of prevailing over a distant adversary, especially it is superior in overall military power, is to prevent it from deploying its forces into the theatre of conflict in the first place.

[46] Ibid, p. 101.

[47] Sergey Sukhankin, "Russia Flexes 'Iskander' Muscles on its Northwestern Flank, *Eurasia Daily Monitor Vol 13 Issue 163*, Jamestown, (12 October 2016), Accessed 01 April 2017,
https://jamestown.org/program/russia-flexes-iskander-muscles-northwestern-flank/

[48] Dave Majumdar, "Biggest Threat US Navy and NATO Face: Russian Subs and A2/AD Bastions", *The National Interest*, (30 June 2016), Accessed 01 April 2017,
http://nationalinterest.org/blog/the-buzz/biggest-threat-us-navy-nato-face-russian-subs-a2-ad-bastions-16808

[49] Ian Brzezinski, Nicholas Varangis, "The NATO-Russia Exercise Gap ... Then, Now, & 2017", *Atlantic Council*, (25 October 2016), Accessed 01 April 2017,
http://www.atlanticcouncil.org/blogs/natosource/the-nato-russia-exercise-gap-then-now-2017

northern partners Sweden and Finland have been in a "strategic time-out" which incorporated massive reductions in capabilities and force postures leaving the North Atlantic and its entrance from the north, the GIUKN-gap[50], wide open (illustrated in Annex 2).[51] Whether NATO's capabilities today can counter the rising military threat of a potent Northern Fleet in the classical warfare areas is at best unclear. Finally, the present NATO Command Structure (NCS) holds some 8,800 posts[52] and needs a continued scrutiny of its relevance to meet today's challenges[53]. With the upcoming introduction of the 'southern hub' at JFC Naples, NATO addresses once more only the potential threats from its Southern Flank.[54]

Authors Hamre and Conley have observed, "Russia has repeatedly demonstrated that it wishes to return to Cold War-era military engagement where it was internationally recognized as a superpower."[55] Since 2001, Russia under Vladimir Putin strived for recognition as the leading maritime power in the North Atlantic. NATO on the other hand took it for granted, that the Atlantic was 'safe' to command. It

---

[50] Greenland, Iceland, UK and Norway Gap. Magnus Nordenman, "Russian Subs Are Reheating a Cold War Chokepoint", *Defense One*, (04 March 2016), Accessed 02 April 2017,
http://www.defenseone.com/ideas/2016/03/russian-subs-are-reheating-cold-war-chokepoint/126428/

[51] *The Military Balance 2017* (London, The International Institute for Strategic Studies, 2017), pp. 63-182.

[52] Background on NATO Command Structure Review, 2011, *NATO*, Accessed 02 April 2017,
http://www.nato.int/nato_static_fl2014/assets/pdf/pdf_2011_06/20110609-Backgrounder_Command_Structure.pdf

[53] Q&A Session at the French MoD during the visit of Senior Course 130 on 27 March 2017.

[54] "Remarks by Secretary Mattis and Secretary-General Stoltenberg at NATO Headquarters, Brussels, Belgium", (15 February 2017), Accessed 02 April 2017,
https://www.defense.gov/News/Speeches/Speech-View/Article/1085050/remarks-by-secretary-mattis-and-secretary-general-stoltenberg-at-nato-headquart

[55] John J Hamre and Heather A Conley, "The Centrality of the North Atlantic to NATO and US Strategic Interests", *Whitehall Papers ,NATO and the North Atlantic, RUSI* (London March 2016), p. 50.

remains questionable, whether Secretary-General Stoltenberg and Secretary of Defense Mattis talk of the same security challenges when one speaks of the fight against terrorism and the setup of a new 'hub for the south' at JFC Naples and the other sees the events of 2014 as 'sobering' and reason to 'adapt'[56]. On the other side, as John Olsen puts it, the Russian Navy today operates in areas and at a tempo not seen for almost two decades.[57]

Russian and new Chinese activities in the North Atlantic should be considered as strategic game changers. In addition, in times of 'fake news' and (maritime) hybrid warfare[58] the critical infrastructures of the North Atlantic (such as oil platforms, offshore installations, underwater communication cables, GPS and satellite communication as well as cruise ships and national minorities) might be targeted.

Overall, the North Atlantic is a vulnerable area that could easily develop into a theatre of operation. It needs to be addressed on a political and military level by the Alliance.

As Julian Lindley-French points out, "Our politicians are suffering from 'Sea-Blindness'. We have to make them aware of the need for maritime/amphibious warfare in the North Atlantic!"[59]

Recommendations

The following recommendations may lead the way to a new cohesive approach to NATO's deterrence and defense posture in the North Atlantic.

---

[56] "Remarks by Secretary Mattis and Secretary-General Stoltenberg at NATO Headquarters, Brussels, Belgium", 15 February 2017, Accessed 02 April 2017, https://www.defense.gov/News/Speeches/Speech-View/Article/1085050/remarks-by-secretary-mattis-and-secretary-general-stoltenberg-at-nato-headquart

[57] John Andreas Olsen, "Introduction: The Quest for Maritime Supremacy", *Whitehall Papers ,NATO and the North Atlantic,* RUSI (London March 2016), p. 5.

[58] James Stravidis, "The United States, The North Atlantic and Maritime Hybrid Warfare", *Whitehall Papers ,NATO and the North Atlantic,* RUSI (London March 2016), pp. 92–101.

[59] Julian Lindley-French, "NATO in the Future", *NATO Defense College*, Committee3 Q&A , 13 April 2017.

a. Winning the narrative

Politicians, military authorities and the (western) European population alike should not be naïve about Russia; its behaviour follows a rational that has been outlined since President Putin took office. Strategic communications of the present threat to the Alliance's security and the need for adequate answers from NATO, specifically on the North Atlantic, should be established.

b. Adapting the Command Structure

NATO is in need for a 'northern hub' to address the challenges of the North Atlantic. Establishing this 'hub' on the western side of the North Atlantic (but within SHAPE) would underline the geostrategic importance of this potential area of operation from a military point of view.

c. Investing Capabilities

The priorities in NATO's Defense Planning Process in the Atlantic domain should be ASW, Anti-Air and A2/AD capabilities. Infrastructure along the former GIUK(N) Gap should be re-invested in and re-opened to be *'fit for purpose'*.

d. Increase Intelligence, Surveillance & Reconnaissance

Apart from recognizing Russia's and China's intentions and strategic engagements in the first place, NATO needs to perceive the potential military threat, in all domains.

e. Increase Exercise & Training

NATO should overcome the exercise gap in quality and quantity to demonstrate its commitment and ability to carry out collective defence in the North Atlantic. An increased "Atlantic Resolve Series"[60] should be the pivot of the exercise and training scheme. The Standing NATO Maritime Group as a high-value asset should constantly be deployed to the North Atlantic and practise high-end, blue-water operations.

---

[60] European Reassurance Initiative (ERI) Fact Sheet, *US DoD*, Accessed 02 April 2017,
https://www.defense.gov/News/Special-Reports/0514_Atlantic-Resolve

Conclusions

The strategic importance of the North Atlantic Ocean and the subsequent challenges have long been underestimated by individual nations and NATO. It can no longer be taken for granted as a benign environment for NATO; available for transit, staging and logistics.

The Russian Federation is following a consistent policy and strategy to establish itself once again as a respected global maritime power. From a Russian standpoint, the North Atlantic is the appropriate domain to achieve this goal. China is yet another global player in the North Atlantic area to be reckoned with. Thus, from a geographical point of view, the notion of 'Atlanticism' needs to find an even stronger place in NATO's strategic thinking both on the political and military level. It would appear that John Andreas Olsen draws a logical conclusion in the following remark: "This 'second coming' in the North Atlantic is the new strategic reality for European security: in broader terms, the 'new Normal'."[61]

The North Atlantic Ocean is as vital to the Alliance as ever and remains the (military) centre of gravity for NATO's collective defence.

---

[61] John Andreas Olsen, "Introduction: The Quest for Maritime Supremacy", *Whitehall Papers*, *NATO and the North Atlantic*, RUSI (London March 2016), p. 6.

Annex: Anti-Submarine Warfare: fixed-wing-aircraft fleets[62]

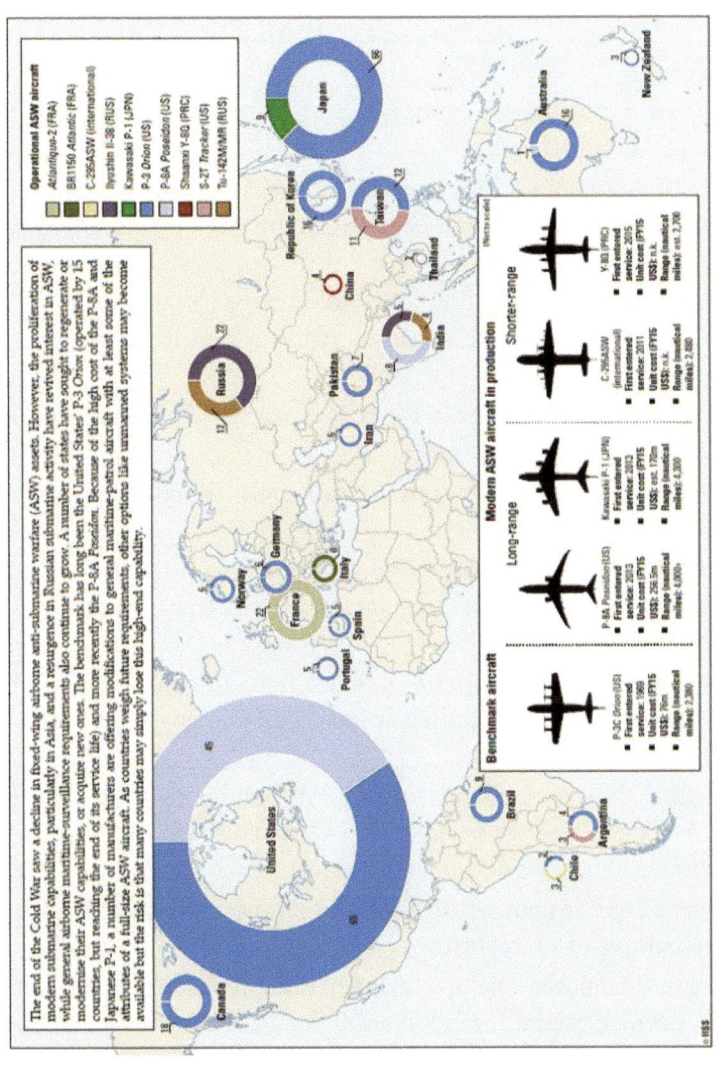

[62] *The Military Balance 2017*, p. 26.

Bibliography

Barlow, Jeffrey G. "NATO's Northern Flank: The growing Soviet threat". *The Heritage Foundation, no.15* (01 May 1979). Accessed 19 March 2017.

http://www.heritage.org/defense/report/natos-northern-flank-the-growing-soviet-threat

Barry, John. "Lessons of Libya for future western military forays". *European Affairs, The European Institute* (August 2011). Accessed 24 April 2017.

https://www.europeaninstitute.org/index.php/130-european-affairs/ea-august-2011/1417-lessons-of-libya-for-future-western-military-forays

Bender, Jeremy. "Business Insider", (01 April 2015), Accessed 06 April 2017.

http://www.businessinsider.com/worlds-eight-oil-chokepoints-2015-4?IR=T

Blair, David. "Russian forces practised invasion of Norway, Finland, Denmark and Sweden", *The Telegraph*, (26 June 2015), Accessed 01 April 2017.

http://www.telegraph.co.uk/news/worldnews/europe/russia/11702328/Russian-forces-practised-invasion-of-Norway-Finland-Denmark-and-Sweden.html

Breum, Martin. "No, Greenland Does Not Belong to China", *The New York Times, The Opinion Page*, (20 February 2013). Accessed 01 April 2017.

http://www.nytimes.com/2013/02/21/opinion/no-greenland-does-not-belong-to-china.html

Breum, Martin. "Analysis: Did the Danish PM prevent a Chinese acquisition on Greenland", *High North News*, (20 December 2016). Accessed 01 April 2017.

http://www.highnorthnews.com/analysis-did-the-danish-pm-prevent-a-chinese-acquisition-on-greenland/

Brzezinski, Ian and Varangis, Nicholas . "The NATO-Russia Exercise Gap … Then, Now, & 2017", *Atlantic Council*, (25 October 2016). Accessed 01 April 2017.

http://www.atlanticcouncil.org/blogs/natosource/the-nato-russia-exercise-gap-then-now-2017

Brezinski, Zbigniew, "On the World: On global politics". *Center for Strategic International Studies, Interview*, (06.October 2015). Accessed 10 April 2017.

https://www.youtube.com/watch?v=7HDBbPzbONM

Clausewitz, Carl von. *On War.* Book 6, (Berlin 1832). Accessed 19 March 2017.

https://www.clausewitz.com/readings/OnWar1873/BK6ch14.html

Frost, David. "BBC Interview with Frost: Vladimir Putin". (05 March 2000). Accessed 20 March 2017.

http://news.bbc.co.uk/hi/english/static/audio_video/programmes/breakfast_with_frost/transcripts/putin5.mar.txt

Frühling, Stephan and Lasconjarias, Guillaume. "NATO, A2/AD and the Kaliningrad Challenge". *Survival Vol 58 No 2*, (May 2016).

Giles, Keir . "The Military Doctrine of the Russian Federation 2010". *Research Review, NATO Defense College* (February 2010).

Hamre, John J and Conley, Heather A. "The Centrality of the North Atlantic to NATO and US Strategic Interests". *Whitehall Papers ,NATO and the North Atlantic*, London: RUSI 2017: 41-58.

Holtsmark, Sven G., "Towards cooperation or confrontation? Security in the High North". *Research Paper No. 45*, NATO Defense College, Rome, February 2009.

Lindley-French, Julian. "NATO in the Future". *NATO Defense College*, Committee3 Q&A. 13 April 2017.

Lulu, Jichang. "China, Greenland and competition fort he Arctic". *China Policy Institute: Analysis*, 02 January 2017. Accessed 01 April 2017.

https://cpianalysis.org/2017/01/02/china-greenland-and-competition-for-the-arctic/

Mahon, Michael K. "Defending Norway and the Northern Flank: Analysis of NATO's Strategic Options". *Naval Postgraduate School* (Monterey 1985): 10-14.

Majumdar, Dave. "Biggest Threat US Navy and NATO Face: Russian Subs and A2/AD Bastions". *The National Interest* (30 June 2016). Accessed 01 April 2017.

http://nationalinterest.org/blog/the-buzz/biggest-threat-us-navy-nato-face-russian-subs-a2-ad-bastions-16808

Nordenman, Magnus. "Russian Subs Are Reheating a Cold War Chokepoint". *Defense One* (04 March 2016), Accessed 02 April 2017.

http://www.defenseone.com/ideas/2016/03/russian-subs-are-reheating-cold-war-chokepoint/126428/

Olsen, John Andreas. "Introduction: The Quest for Maritime Supremacy". *Whitehall Papers ,NATO and the North Atlantic*, London: RUSI 2017: 3-7.

Pettersen, Trude. "Plans to reopen military base on Kola Peninsula". *Barents Observer*, 21 February 2014, Accessed 01 April 2014.

http://barentsobserver.com/en/security/2014/02/plans-reopen-military-base-kola-peninsula-21-02

Pukov, Ruslan. "Russia's Naval Doctrine: New Priorities and Benchmarks". *Valdai Club*, 17 August 2015.

http://valdaiclub.com/a/highlights/russia_s_naval_doctrine_new_priorities_and_benchmarks/

Søreide, Ine Erikson. "NATO and the North Atlantic, Revitalizing Collective Defense and the Maritime Domain". *PRISM 6, No.2*, Center for Complex Operations (CCO) at the National Defense University (3 August 2016): 49-57.

Strange, Joseph L. and Iron, Richard. "Center of Gravity; What Clausewitz Really Meant". *Joint Force Quarterly 35*, NDU, (October 2004), 20 – 27.

Stravidis, James. "The United States, The North Atlantic and Maritime Hybrid Warfare". *Whitehall Papers ,NATO and the North Atlantic*, London: RUSI 2017: 92-101.

Sukhankin, Sergey. "Russia Flexes 'Iskander' Muscles on its Northwestern Flank". *Eurasia Daily Monitor Vol 13 Issue 163*, Jamestown (12 October 2016). Accessed 01 April 2017.

https://jamestown.org/program/russia-flexes-iskander-muscles-northwestern-flank/

Zolotukhina, Elizabeth. "Can Russia Implement its New Naval Doctrine". *Centre for Geopolitics & Security in Realism Studies*, 03 August 2015.

"European Reassurance Initiative (ERI) Fact Sheet". *US DoD*. Accessed 02 April 2017.

https://www.defense.gov/News/Special-Reports/0514_Atlantic-Resolve

"Maritime Doctrine of the Russian Federation 2020, Approved by President Vladimir Putin (27 July 2001)". Accessed 20 March 2017.

http://www.oceanlaw.org/downloads/arctic/Russian_Maritime_Policy_2020.pdf

"The Military Doctrine of the Russian Federation, Approved by Russian Federation presidential edict (5 February 2010), II 8. The main external military dangers". Accessed 20 March 2017.

http://carnegieendowment.org/files/2010russia_military_doctrine.pdf

"The Military Balance 2017". The International Institute for Strategic Studies, London. 2017. 63-182.

"Russian explorers have planted their country's flag on the seabed 4,200m (14,000ft) below the North Pole to further Moscow's claims to the Arctic." *BBC News*. Accessed 19 March 2017.

http://news.bbc.co.uk/2/hi/europe/6927395.stm

"Russia simulated an attack on Denmark". *The Local dk* (31 October 2014), Accessed 01 April 2017.

https://www.thelocal.dk/20141031/russia-simulated-a-military-attack-on-denmark

NATO:

"Active Engagement, Modern Defence", Strategic Concept. (19 November 2010).

"Allied Command Operations, Comprehensive Operations Planning Directive Interim V2.0". (04 October 2013).

"Background on NATO Command Structure Review, 2011". Accessed 02 April 2017.

http://www.nato.int/nato_static_fl2014/assets/pdf/pdf_2011_06/20110609-Backgrounder_Command_Structure.pdf

"Founding Act on Mutual Relations, Cooperation and Security between NATO and the Russian Federation". (27 May 1997). Accesses 24 April 2017.

http://www.nato.int/cps/en/natohq/official_texts_25468.htm

"NATO Glossary of Terms and Definition", AAP-06 Edition 2014.

"NATO Handbook". (29 October 2002). Accessed 19 March 2017.

https://web.archive.org/web/20080813225955/http://www.nato.int/docu/handbook/2001/hb120704.htm

"NATO-Russia Council Joint Statement". (20 November 2010). Accessed 24 April 2017.

http://www.nato.int/cps/en/natohq/news_68871.htm

"NATO Tracks large-Scale Russian Air Activity in Europe". (20 October 2014). Accessed 01 April 2017.

http://www.shape.nato.int/nato-tracks-largescale-russian-air-activity-in-europe

"North Atlantic Military Committee Decision on M.C. 14/1, 9". (December 1952). Accessed 06 April 2017.

http://www.nato.int/docu/stratdoc/eng/a521209a.pdf

„Preamble to the North Atlantic Treaty (1949)". Accessed 10 April 2017

http://www.nato.int/cps/en/natohq/official_texts_17120.htm

"Remarks by Secretary Mattis and Secretary-General Stoltenberg at NATO Headquarters, Brussels, Belgium". (15 February 2017). Accessed 02 April 2017.
https://www.defense.gov/News/Speeches/Speech-View/Article/1085050/remarks-by-secretary-mattis-and-secretary-general-stoltenberg-at-nato-headquart

„The strategic concept for the defence of the North Atlantic Area, D.C. 6/1". (01 December 1949). Accessed 06 April 2017.
http://www.nato.int/docu/stratdoc/eng/a491201a.pdf

"Wales Summit Declaration". (05 September 2014). Accessed 19 March 2017
http://www.nato.int/cps/en/natohq/official_texts_112964.htm?mode=pressrelease

"Warsaw Summit Communiqué", (09 July 2016). Accessed 19 March 2017.
http://www.nato.int/cps/en/natohq/official_texts_133169.htm

Willi Bentzinger
Is Russia Still a Technological Power?

Introduction
This article deals with Russia's capabilities in the area of technology. Starting from an analysis of Russia's current situation of its economic power, specific areas of Russia's technological prowess are being analyzed.

Could Russia retain his former status as a superpower?
In a news conference at the end of 2016 the former President of the United States (US) Barack Obama stated "The Russians can't change us or significantly weaken us. They are a smaller country, they are a weaker country, their economy doesn't produce anything that anybody wants to buy except oil and gas and arms. They don't innovate".[1] Is this statement in accordance with the facts? The following analysis will shed light on various aspects of this question with emphasis on the technological topic.

Economy
Russia's economy is roughly the size of Italy or Canada and is dependent on oil and gas revenues.[2] Since sanctions have been imposed on Russia after the annexation of Crimea and the intervention in Ukraine and due to the concurrent decline of oil prices, Russia is trying to overcome a recession.

---

[1] Barack Obama, "Russia is smaller, weaker country", *CNBC video*, Friday 16 Dec 2016, http://video.cnbc.com/gallery/?video=3000577041.

[2] Larisa Epatko, "Once a superpower, how strong is Russia now?", *PBS Newshour*, January 13, 2017, pp. 1-13, http://www.pbs.org/newshour/updates/how-strong-is-russia-now/

Private sector

The attempt of the government to control this sector constrains the emergence of innovative start-up companies, like in the US and in European countries, with detrimental effect on economic progress.

Gross Domestic Product (GDP) ranking

According to estimates of the World Bank in 2015, Russia was number 13 with the US in the first position and China in the second.[3]

Russia's space program

The space programs of the former Soviet Union had a long lasting tradition commencing in the late 50s.[4] The first satellite in orbit was the Russian "Sputnik", the first man in space was Yuri Gagarin followed by the first woman in space, Valentina Tereshkova. However, the Soviets lost the moon race in 1969. Nevertheless, they continued their programs, in particular regarding long-term missions in their space-stations "Mir" and "Salyut" thus gaining continuous experience and expertise.[5] The Cold War competition changed to cooperation after the collapse of the Soviet Union. Russia supported, to a great extent, the International Space Station (ISS).

A characteristic element of exploring space is that scientists and engineers from many countries worldwide work together. This is reflected by the National Aeronautics and Space Administration's (NASA) success which is based on cooperation with a wide number of space agencies. For example, the ISS has been operated by US, Russian, Japanese, Canadian and European space agencies for more than 16 years. 18 nations have sent their astronauts into the orbit who conducted experiments of 93 countries.[6]

---

[3] Ibid., p. 6.

[4] Ellen Stofan, "When We Explore Space, We Go Together", *SLATE*, March 7 2017, accessed 2 May 2017,
http://slate.com/articles/technology/future_tense/2017/03/space_exploration_re quires_international _collaboration.html.

[5] Ibid.

[6] Ibid.

Currently, the explorations of Mars and the Moon are on top of the program list. However, no country has the financial, technological and scientific resources to achieve these goals alone.[7]

In addition, the use of the Earth-observing satellites provides another area of international cooperation, particular in the field of humanitarian crises and natural disasters when these instruments are capable and needed to support rescue and recovery missions.[8]

Certainly there are other space programs driven by military requirements.

Russia uses a variety of satellites for military purposes.[9]

- Early warning
- Signal intelligence
- Optical reconnaissance
- Positioning, Navigation and Timing (PNT)
- Communication

The whole spectrum is mainly based on improved, advanced and upgraded already existing systems from the former Soviet Union. Many of these systems have a dual-use character. For example, the navigation system which makes Russia independent from the US Global Positioning System (GPS) is their Global Navigation Satellite System (GLONASS), which is being used by both the military and the civil sides. The history of GLONASS also reflects Russia's early engagement in space programs.

---

[7] Ibid.

[8] Ibid.

[9] Jana Honkova, "The Russian Federation's Approach to Military Space and its Military Space Capacities", Russian Military Space, *George C. Marshall Institute*, November 2013, p 10. http://marshall.org/wp-content/uploads/2013/11/Russian-Space-Nov-13.pdf.

The first ideas to use satellites for navigation were developed already in 1957.[10] Following continuous development and significant improvements of this technology, the GLONASS program was started in 1982 with the aim to place 24 satellites in orbit. However, funding difficulties in 1990 set back the program. In 2002, only seven satellites were available, insufficient for navigation.[11] Based on a revised long term program from 2002-2011 the GLONASS satellite system is now supposed to be operational. It needs to be stressed that capability enhancements of the GLONASS system is mostly driven by the space segment. An additional ambitious sustainment program scheduled for 2012-2020 shall not only demonstrate that Russia is able to compete with other international satellite systems but also strives for taking the leadership in satellite navigation technology.[12]

Cyber Warfare

Cyber attacks are characterized by:

- Border crossing activities,
- being part of hybrid warfare,
- Actors (non-state and state actors) very hard or impossible to identify.

---

[10] "GLONASS History", Information and Analysis Center for Positioning, Navigation and Timing, 2005-2017, Korolyov, Russia, https://www.glonass-iac.ru/en/guide/.

[11] Ibid.

[12] Ibid.

Due to this increasing threat, the North Atlantic Treaty Organization (NATO) added cyberspace as an additional operational domain in the Warsaw summit in 2016 to the existing domains of air, land and sea.[13] In a conflict, cyber attacks are used to achieve diplomatic and military objectives. For this purpose, cyber weapons are being developed and applied as they have the potential to cause damage and harm to a nation's infrastructure and even human beings.[14] Moreover, cyber attacks have the capability to manipulate societies by influencing the public opinion and to destabilize nations. Russia's military admitted that they have significantly expanded their efforts in this area since the end of the Cold War and NATO would be a top target.[15]

Although there is no court-type evidence yet, Russia is being accused by the US of having turned the presidential election in favour of Donald Trump in 2016 by hacking the email account of Hillary Clinton, the candidate of the Democratic Party.[16]

Another major incident, which underpins the skillfulness and highly sophisticated capability of launching a cyber attack against the governmental infrastructure of a country, was the attack against the German Parliament in 2015.[17] A group of hackers spied on the computer network of the parliament for weeks and downloaded a huge amount of private and confidential data from several Members of Parliament. There is evidence that suggest Russia as the originator but again this evidence, based on the analysis of the infiltrated malware, cannot be used as official proof. However, it is interesting to note that all these attacks serve to implement Russia's foreign policy interests and goals.

---

[13] Jens Stoltenberg, "NATO and Cyber: Time to raise our game", *Defense News*, July 8, 2016,
http://www.defensenews.com/story/defense/omr/roadtowarsaw/2016/07/08/nato-and-cyber-time-raise-our-game/86859198/.

[14] Tim Stevens, "Cyberweapons: An Emerging Global Governance Architecture ", January 2017, *Palgrave Communications, Vol. 3, 2017*, p. 2,
https://papers.ssrn.com/sol3/papers.cfm?abstract_id=2897454

[15] BBC News, "Russian military admits significant cyberwar effort", 23 February 2017, http://www.bbc.com/news/world-europe-39062663

[16] Ibid.

[17] Patrick Beuth, Kai Biermann, Martin Klingst, Holger Stark, "Merkel und der schicke Bär", *Die Zeit*, 11.05.2017.

There is, however, another battlefield which Russia should not underestimate. Russia is also a potential target of attacks carried out by criminals. On Sunday 17 May 2017, the New York Times reported of an international cyber attack that demanded ransom from the infected users otherwise their data would remain encrypted[18] and thus useless. Among the governments affected was the Russian Interior Ministry, which confirmed that 1000 of its computers had been infected. This international attack hit hospitals in the UK, companies in Spain and Germany and other countries but according to the New York Times, Russia was hit worst.

The Russian Army

Defence budget

Russia's defence budget for 2017 is being cut by about 5%, which may jeopardize Russia's official goal to have modernized 70% of its forces by 2020.[19] However, Russia spends about a third of the total budget for defence and other security related services.[20] This share needs to be considered in relation to 2.3% for health and 3.5% for education.[21] On the other hand, this huge amount of money keeps the defence industry alive especially in regions, which mostly rely on and whose economy is dependent on the bulk of military and security orders.[22]

---

[18] Russell Goldman, "What We Know and Don't Know About the International Cyberattack", *The New York Times,* May 12, 2017,
https://www.nytimes.com/2017/05/12/world/europe/international-cyberattack-ransomware.html?_r=0

[19] Mark Galeotti, "The truth about Russia's defence budget", *European Council on Foreign Relations,* 24th March, 2017,
http:www.ecfr.eu/article/commentary_the_truth_about_russias_defence_budget_7255

[20] Ibid.

[21] Ibid.

[22] Ibid.

Military Power

First reforms of the Russian Army started in 2000 after the First Chechen War 1994-1996 when the poor performance, the inefficiencies and corruption of the Army became evident.[23] It happened when Boris Yeltsin handed over power to Vladimir Putin at the end of 1999, who at that time was still Prime Minister before he was elected President in 2000. Apart from the restructuring of the forces that aims to a leaner and more effective military, Putin has started a modernization programme of the military inventory. In 2000, Putin pledged to spend the equivalent of US $650 billion until 2020.[24] Despite many problems due to corruption and embezzlement, Russia proceeds to generate a modern force, which has already been demonstrated in Ukraine and Syria.

Amongst a variety of improvements, two technological areas are being considered in more detail: the advanced surface-to-air missile systems (SAM) and the unmanned air vehicles (UAV). It needs to be emphasized that an assessment of the nuclear power of Russia is outside the scope of this article.

Russia's surface-to-air missile systems

The air defence capability of the Russian forces came into public in July 2014 when a medium-range surface-to-air missile (BUK) shot down the Malayan Airlines flight MH17 over the Donbas.[25]

---

[23] Mark Galeotti, "The Modern Russian Army 1992-2016", 2017 *Osprey Publishing Ltd.*, pp. 11-63.

[24] Ibid., p. 34.

[25] Ibid., p. 62.

However, this is only an indication of Russia's capabilities in this sector. Russia has not only continued developing powerful air defence systems but also has initiated the replacement of all its "strategic" and long range SAM missiles as part of their modernization programme. As a result, it is expected that Russia will establish an integrated air-defence network that will encompass the S-500, S-400, S-300 and S-350 weapon systems.[26]

Russia has deployed S-400 missiles in Kaliningrad capable to defend the airspace over the Baltic states and to a great extent also over Polish territory.[27]

The S-400 system and its most advanced interceptor missile, designed for direct hit, covers a range up to 65 nm and has an altitude capability up to 100 kft.[28] The capability of the missile to sustain turn rates of 60g at sea level and 20g at 30000m enables a direct kill endgame against ballistic and high speed targets, which include even guided missiles. Due to its improvements in applied radar and antenna technologies, Electronic Counter Measures and software upgrades, the S-400 system is intended to intercept aerial vehicles such as stand-off jammer aircraft, AWACS aircraft, reconnaissance aircraft and armed strategic bombers.[29]

---

[26] Dave Majumbar, "S-500: Russia's Super Weapon That Could Kill the B-2, F-22, or F-35?", *The National Interest*, April 10 2017, http://nationalinterest.org/blog/the-buzz/s-500-russias-super-weapon-could-kill-the-b-2-f-22-or-f-35-20107

[27] Sebastien Roblin, "Forget About Russia's S-300 or S-400 (The S-500 Is Coming)", http://nationalinterest.org/blog/the-buzz/forget-about-russias s-300-or-s-400-the-s-500-coming-20560

[28] Dr Carlo Kopp, "Almaz-Antey 40R6/S-400 Triumf Self Propelled Air Defence System/SA-21", *Air Power Australia*, Technical Report APA-TR-2009-0503, May 2009, Updated April 2012

[29] Ibid.

The delivery of the first samples of the S-500 anti-aircraft missile system is considered imminent. This powerful new weapon shall be able to engage targets at about 125 miles altitude, high enough to attack ballistic missiles in space. The S-500 system shall be stowed in special containers, which provides a shield against being detected by satellites and will use secured communication links against electronic warfare.[30]

The S-400 air defence system is also foreseen for the export market. Following negotiations with India and China, also the NATO member state Turkey is going to procure the system. On 12 September 2017 BBC NEWS reported that Turkey had signed this deal.[31] Certainly, these deals would contribute to the overall weapons exports which make Russia number 2 in the value of all arms deliveries worldwide.[32] This means money, which is urgently needed by the Russian economy.

---

[30] Sebastien Roblin, "Forget About Russia's S-300 or S-400 (The S-500 Is Coming)", http://nationalinterest.org/blog/the-buzz/forget-about-russias s-300-or-s-400-the-s-500-coming-20560

[31] "Turkey signs deal to get Russian S-400 air defence missiles", *BBC NEWS*, 12. Sept 2017,
http://www.bbc.com/news/world-europe-41237812

[32] Christopher Woody, "The US and Russia are dominating the global weapons trade", Business Insider: Military & Defense, Dec 28, 2016.

Unmanned Air Vehicles

In the Second Chechen War (1999-2002), small drones developed for surveillance and observation supported Russia's helicopters and artillery. Equipped with crude sensors Russia's backwardness became evident during the Georgian War in 2008. Since then, Russia has intensified its endeavours to catch up by reinforcing research and also by considering procurement of drones. Consequently, significant progress has been achieved although Russia has not been in a position to present an armed Unmanned Air Vehicle (UAV) up to now. Russia still does not reach the technological level of the NATO member states in particular in the Medium Altitude Long Endurance / High Altitude Long Endurance class (MALE / HALE) as essential equipment and suitable weapons are missing.[33] But certainly this is only a question of time as the Russian MoD has committed to spend about $9 billion on military UAVs by 2020. Nevertheless, Russia has already (and this is interesting to note) developed a strategy on how to use UAVs and robots technology in an armed conflict. That could be an indication that Russia is putting more and more focus on no-contact warfare.

Conclusion and Recommendations

In order to find an answer to the question raised at the beginning of the document: "Is Russia still a technological superpower?", dedicated technology fields were analyzed taking into account the current economic conditions. Indeed, there are specific areas where Russia is at least on par with NATO member states. Since Vladimir Putin has adopted power, the economic situation within the country has improved, although it is a slow-moving process. This is reflected by the following statistical data. Still behind the US (almost 80 years) and even China (78 years), Russia's life expectancy increased from 64.5 years in 1993 to 70 years in 2010.[34] Despite the fact that Russia spends a considerable share of its GDP to modernize and upgrade its

---

[33] Mark Galeotti, "The Modern Russian Army", p. 63.

[34] Larisa Epatko, "Once a superpower, how strong is Russia now?", *PBS Newshour*, January 13, 2017, p. 4, http://www.pbs.org/newshour/updates/how-strong-is-russia-now/

military inventory, Russia still lacks in high-tech products. In October 2016, two Russian nationals and one citizen of the US were arrested as they were suspected in illegally exporting controlled microelectronics technology from the US to Russia.[35]

Amongst the investigated weapon systems, UAV and SAM, only the S-400 and S-500 surface-to-air missiles are powerful and outstanding weapons. Concerning the UAV technology, Russia is definitely behind NATO and in particular the US.

It needs to be highlighted that Russia considers themselves on par with foreign developments in the field of space systems.[36] This position is supported by a lecture, presented at ESRIN on 19 May 2017. A comparison of the capabilities between Russia and NATO in the areas of PNT, space based intelligence, surveillance and reconnaissance (ISR), satellite communication (SATCOM) and launch capabilities showed that both parties are considered strong and comparable.[37] In addition, Russia continues with its ambitious space exploration program, which, however, cannot be carried out alone. Concerning cyberspace, Russia is certainly a main player.[38]

---

[35] Department of Justice, "Brooklyn Resident and Two Russian Nationals Arrested in Connection with Scheme to Illegally Export Controlled Technology to Russia", *Justice News*, Thursday, October 6, 2016,
https://www.justice.gov/opa/pr/brooklyn-resident-and-two-russian-nationals-arrested-connection scheme-illegally-export

[36] L. Gokhberg (Ed.) (2016), "Russia 2030: Science and Technology Foresight". Ministry of Education and Science of the Russian Federation, National Research University Higher School of Economics. p. 168,
https://lsts.hse.ru/en/news/173582352.html.

[37] Laryssa Patten, "Space and its significance for Defense and Security", Lecture at ESRIN, 19 May 2017.

[38] This was highlighted and confirmed by Dr. Gaythan during a lecture at the NATO Defense College in Rome. Dr. Sandro Gaycken, "Cyber Warfare and Defence", *Lecture at the NDC*, May 16, 2017.

Based on these results, Michael McFaul's statement that Russia is not a superpower (Michael McFaul was the former US ambassador to Russia)[39] may apply to an overall assessment of Russia's power including the area of technology, but Russia will continue with its military modernization programs. Additionally, both, the civil and the military space projects including missile defence and in particular the cyber warfare capabilities are of considerable importance for Russia that makes this nation to a serious opponent.

Consequently, two potential areas have been identified for cooperation with Russia:

- space exploration
- cyberspace protection

The first bullet not only relates to the use of space in order to achieve progress in science but also contributes to push the economy by fostering the commercial sector whilst generating new business models.

The rationale behind the second bullet is based on the assumption that cooperation in this area with other stakeholders should be in Russia's own interest. Even Russia is not protected against cyber attacks from non-state actors with no military background, which may result in a catastrophic effect in their country.

---

[39] Steve Inskeep et al, "What kind of threat does Russia pose to the US", *PBS Newshour*, Januar 12, 2017, http://www.pbs.org/newshour/bb/kind-threat-russia-pose-u-s/

Bibliography

BBC News. "Russian military admits significant cyberwar effort". 23 February 2017.

http://www.bbc.com/news/world-europe-39062663.

BBC News. "Turkey signs deal to get Russian S-400 air defence missiles". 12 September 2017.

http://www.bbc.com/news/world-europe-41237812

Beuth, Patrick, Biermann, Kai,Klingst,Martin, Stark,Holger. "Merkel und der schicke Bär. *Die Zeit.* 11.05.2017.

Department of Justice. "Brooklyn Resident and Two Russian Nationals Arrested in Connection with Scheme to Illegally Export Controlled Technology to Russia". *Justice News*, Thursday, October 6, 2016. https://www.justice.gov/opa/pr/brooklyn-resident-and-two-russian-nationals-arrested-connection scheme-illegally-export.

Epatko, Larisa. "Once a superpower, how strong is Russia now?". *PBS Newshour*, January 13, 2017, pp. 1-13.

http://www.pbs.org/newshour/updates/how-strong-is-russia-now/.

Galeotti, Mark "The truth about Russia's defence budget". *European Council on Foreign Relations.* 24th March, 2017.

http:www.ecfr.eu/article/commentary_the_truth_about_russias_defence_budget_7255

Galeotti, Mark. "The Modern Russian Army 1992-2016". 2017 *Osprey Publishing Ltd.*, pp. 1- 63.

Gaycken, Dr., Sandro. "Cyber Warfare and Defence", *Lecture at the NDC*, May 16, 2017

"GLONASS History". Information and Analysis Center for Positioning, Navigation and Timing, 2005-2017. Korolyov, Russia. https://www.glonass-iac.ru/en/guide/.

Gokhberg L. (Ed.) (2016) Russia 2030: Science and Technology Foresight. Ministry of Education and Science of the Russian Federation. National Research University Higher School of Economics. 1-132. https://lsts.hse.ru/en/news/173582352.html.

Goldman, Russell. "What We Know and Don't Know About the International Cyberattack". *The New York Times.* May 12, 2017. https://www.nytimes.com/2017/05/12/world/europe/international-cyberattack-ransomware.html?_r=0

Honkova, Jana. "The Russian Federation's Approach to Military Space and its Military Space Capacities". Russian Military Space. *George C. Marshall Institute* , November 2013. 1-42. http://marshall.org/wp-content/uploads/2013/11/Russian-Space-Nov-13.pdf.

Inskeep, Steve, Mattis, Gen (Ret.), James, Farkas, Evelyn,Obama, Barack, McFaul, Michael,Trump, Donald. "What kind of threat does Russia pose to the US". *PBS Newshour,* Januar 12, 2017. http://www.pbs.org/newshour/bb/kind-threat-russia-pose-u-s/ content/uploads/2013/11/Russian-Space-Nov-13.pdf.

Kopp, Dr., Carlo. "Almaz-Antey 40R6/S-400 Triumf Self Propelled Air Defence System/SA-21". *Air Power Australia.* Technical Report APA-TR-2009-0503, May 2009. Updated April, 2012.

Majumbar, Dave. "S-500: Russia's Super Weapon That Could Kill the B-2, F-22, or F-35?". *The National Interest.* April 10 2017. http://nationalinterest.org/blog/the-buzz/s-500-russias-super-weapon-could-kill-the-b-2-f-22-or-f-35-20107.

Obama, Barack. "Russia is smaller, weaker country". *CNBC video,* Friday 16 Dec 2016.

http://video.cnbc.com/gallery/?video=3000577041.

Patten, Laryssa. "Space and its significance for Defense and Security". Lecture at ESRIN, Frascati, 19 May 2017.

Roblin, Sebastien. " Forget About Russia's S-300 or S-400 (The S-500 Is Coming)". http://nationalinterest.org/blog/the-buzz/forget-about-russias s-300-or-s-400-the-s-500-coming-20560.

Stevens, Tim. "Cyberweapons: An Emerging Global Governance Architecture ". January 2017. *Palgrave Communications, Vol. 3, 2017.* pp. 1-6.

https://papers.ssrn.com/sol3/papers.cfm?abstract_id=2897454.

Stofan, Ellen. "When We Explore Space, We Go Together". *SLATE*, March 7 2017. Accessed 2 May 2017.

http://slate.com/articles/technology/future_tense/2017/03/space_exploration_requires_international_collaboration.html.

Stoltenberg, Jens. "NATO and Cyber: Time to raise our game". *Defense News*, July 8 2016.

http://www.defensenews.com/story/defense/omr/roadtowarsaw/2016/07/08/nato-and-cyber-time-raise-our-game/86859198/.

Woody, Christopher. "The US and Russia are dominating the global weapons trade". Business Insider: Military & Defense, Dec 28, 2016.

Jan Ballast
Transatlantic Intelligence Cooperation. Strengthening NATO's First Line of Defense[1]

Introduction

On 21 October 2016, the North Atlantic Treaty Organization (NATO) appointed its first Assistant Secretary General for Intelligence and Security (ASG-I&S), Dr. Arndt Freiherr Freytag von Loringhoven.[2] His appointment was the result of a meeting of the North Atlantic Council (NAC) on 8-9 July 2016 in Warsaw, where the Heads of State and Government stated the requirement to strengthen intelligence within NATO.[3] In doing so, the Alliance underlined that improved cooperation on intelligence would increase early warning, force protection and general resilience.[4]

NATO's new intelligence chief, a former German ambassador and Vice President of the Bundesnachrichtendienst (BND), is responsible

---

[1] This article was earlier presented at the NATO Defense College, Rome, Italy, in May 2017. The unabridged version of this article was published by NATO Defense College as a Research Paper in September 2017, see: Jan Ballast, "Trust (in) NATO - The future of intelligence sharing within the Alliance", *NATO Defense College Research Paper,* no. 140 (September 2017): pp. 1-16. The views expressed here are the author's and do not necessarily reflect those of NATO or the NATO Defense College.

[2] "Deutscher wird erster Geheimdienst-Chef der NATO", *RP Online*, 21 October 2016. Accessed 13 May 2017. http://www.rp-online.de/politik/ausland/deutscher-arndt-freytag-von-loringhoven-wird-erster-geheimdienstchef-der-nato-aid-1.6342986; Julian Barnes, "NATO Appoints Its First Intelligence Chief", *Wall Street Journal,* 21 October 2016. Accessed 13 May 2017.
https://www.wsj.com/articles/nato-appoints-its-first-intelligence-chief-1477070563

[3] "Warsaw Summit Communiqué Issued by the Heads of State and Government participating in the meeting of the North Atlantic Council in Warsaw 8-9 July 2016, 09 Jul. 2016, Press Release (2016) 100". *NATO.* Accessed 13 May 2017. http://www.nato.int/cps/en/natohq/official_texts_133169.htm

[4] Ibidem; Jamie Shea, "Resilience: a core element of collective defence", *NATO Review Magazine*, 2016. Accessed 13 May 2017.
http://www.nato.int/docu/review/2016/Also-in-2016/nato-defence-cyberresilience/EN/index.htm

for setting up a new joint intelligence and security division at HQ level. This will merge both military and civilian intelligence pillars, providing intelligence support to the NAC, NATO's senior political decision-making body, and the Military Committee (MC), the Alliance's senior military authority. It will also advise the Secretary General (SG) on intelligence and security matters.[5]

This paper assesses the future of sharing intelligence within NATO following the appointment of the ASG-I&S. It outlines the views of different experts on intelligence cooperation and what sharing of secrets within a multinational organization means. Subsequently, NATO's intelligence structure is analyzed, including previous proposals meant to improve intelligence collaboration. The paper continues by identifying the more challenging aspects of intelligence cooperation facing the ASG-I&S, and his do's and don'ts concerning structure, sharing and content are discussed. Based on theory and practice, six recommendations are made with the aim of enabling Freytag von Loringhoven and his joint division a proposal to enhance intelligence as the first line of defense of the Alliance, with obvious benefits in terms of resilience.

Sharing secrets

Scholars on intelligence fundamentally agree that states and their national intelligence and security services are reluctant to share sensitive, classified information with international organizations and favor cooperation on a bilateral, case-by-case basis.[6] In fact, intelligence is shared only when there is a common threat perception, mutual trust, a demonstrable added value, the right type of diplomatic relationships

---

[5] "Ex-BND-Vize übernimmt Geheimdienstposten bei NATO", *n-tv*, 24 October 2016. Accessed 13 May 2017. http://www.n-tv.de/ticker/Ex-BND-Vize-uebernimmt-Geheimdienstposten-bei-Nato-article18921376.html

[6] Stéphane Lefebvre, "The Difficulties and Dilemmas of International Intelligence Cooperation", *International Journal of Intelligence and CounterIntelligence* 16, no. 4 (2003), 527-529; Joseph W. Wippl, "Intelligence Exchange Through InterIntel", *International Journal of Intelligence and CounterIntelligence* 25, no. 11 (2012), p. 8.

or a combination of incentives.⁷ The most successful bilateral secret intelligence collaboration is the Anglo-American UKUSA Agreement, originally signed in 1946, which evolved into the exclusive multilateral so-called 'Five Eyes' cooperation.⁸

Examples of beneficial intelligence cooperation by states within international organizations, such as NATO, are much harder to find. From the outset Member States shared secret information bilaterally on political and military issues with NATO; however, major countries within the Alliance, afraid of the non-secure Brussels bureaucracy, kept intelligence from other Members.⁹ Chris Clough warned that "within recent military coalitions, intelligence-contributing nations have been mindful of the dangers of compromise by less security-conscious partners, while knowing that a degree of sharing is essential."¹⁰

Some argue that international institutions like NATO play a major role in encouraging and facilitating intelligence sharing among their member states.¹¹ Although "even in the UN intelligence is no longer

---

⁷ Lefebvre, "The Difficulties and Dilemmas", p. 529; Chris Clough, "Quid Pro Quo: The Challenges of International Strategic Intelligence Cooperation", *International Journal of Intelligence and CounterIntelligence* 17, no. 4 (2004), p. 605; Cees Wiebes, "De problemen rond de internationale intelligence liaison", *Justitiële Verkenningen* 30, no. 3 (2004), pp. 79-80; Derek S. Reveron, "Old Allies, New Friends: Intelligence Sharing in the War of Terror", *Orbis* 50, no. 3 (Summer 2006), p. 457; Monica Den Boer, "Counter-Terrorism, Security and Intelligence in the EU: Governance Challenges for Collection, Exchange and Analysis", *Intelligence and National Security* 30, no. 2-3 (2015), p. 404.

⁸ See for the UKUSA Agreement between the First Party (the United States) and Second Parties (the UK, Australia, Canada and New Zealand): Richard J. Aldrich, "British Intelligence and the Anglo-American 'Special Relationship' during the Cold War," *Review of International Studies*, Vol. 24, No. 1, March 1998, pp. 331-351; James Igoe Walsh, *The International Politics of Intelligence Sharing* (New York: Columbia University Press, 2009), pp. 31-44; Adam D. M. Svendsen, *Intelligence Cooperation and the War on Terror: Anglo-American Security Relations After 9/11* (London and New York: Routledge, 2010).

⁹ Clough, "Quid Pro Quo", 604; Don Munton and Karima Fredj, "Sharing Secrets: A Game Theoretic Analysis of International Intelligence Cooperation", *International Journal of Intelligence and CounterIntelligence* 26, no. 4 (2013), p. 673.

¹⁰ Clough, "Quid Pro Quo", p. 602.

a dirty word",[12] others remain of the opinion that nations are unable to overcome mistrust, making them reluctant to engage in multilateral intelligence cooperation.[13]

The focus of the intelligence world changed profoundly following 9/11 with the emergence of counterterrorism (CT) and non-state actors as dominating global themes.[14] On a multilateral level, NATO, lacking its own sources by design, responded by introducing intelligence liaison and fusion elements and reaffirming its commitment to intelligence sharing.[15] However, different languages, cultures, capabili-

---

[11] Simon Duke, "Intelligence, security and information flows in CFSP", *Intelligence and National Security* 21, no. 4 (2006), p. 624; Adam Svendsen, "The globalization of intelligence since 9/11: Frameworks and operational parameters", *Cambridge Review of International Affairs* 21, no. 1 (2008), p. 133; Martin J. Ara, Thomas Brand and Brage A. Larssen, *Help A Brother Out: A Case Study in Multinational Intelligence Sharing, NATO SOF* (Monterey: Naval Postgraduate School, December 2011), p. 45; Daniel G. Pronk, "Sharing the Burden, Sharing the Secrets. The Fulcrum of Transatlantic Intelligence Cooperation", draft for Conference "Creating and Challenging the Transatlantic Intelligence Community" presented at Woodrow Wilson International Center for Scholars, 30 March-1 April 2017, p. 2.

[12] Briefing by Maj Gen Adrian Foster, UN Deputy Military Adviser, UN HQ, New York, 11 May 2017.

[13] Lefebvre, "The Difficulties and Dilemmas", 537; Richard J. Aldrich, "Transatlantic Intelligence and Security Cooperation", *International Affairs* 80, no 4 (2004), 737; Clough, "Quid Pro Quo", 612; Björn Fägersten, "For EU eyes only? Intelligence and European security", *European Union Institute for Security Studies,* Brief no. 8 (March 2016), pp. 2-3.

[14] Patrick F. Walsh and Seumas Miller, "Rethinking 'Five Eyes' Security Intelligence Collection Policies and Practice Post Snowden", *Intelligence and National Security* 31, no. 3 (2016), p. 357.

[15] "Prague Summit Declaration Issued by the Heads of State and Government of the North Atlantic Council in Prague on 21 November 2002". *NATO.* Accessed 13 May 2017. http://www.nato.int/docu/pr/2002/p02-127e.htm; "Istanbul Summit Communiqué Issued by the Heads of State and Government of the North Atlantic Council, Press Release (2004)096, 28 June 2004". *NATO.* Accessed 13 May 2017. http://www.nato.int/docu/pr/2004/p04-096e.htm; John R. Deni, "Beyond Information Sharing: NATO and the Foreign Fighter Threat", *Parameters* 45, no. 2 (Summer 2015), pp. 55-57.

ties and infrastructures proved to be structural constraints.[16]

Intelligence within the Alliance

Until the appointment of the ASG-I&S in October 2016, political-strategic intelligence in NATO HQ was divided between civilian and military pillars, despite the Alliance already agreeing in 2004 in Istanbul to "a review of current intelligence structures".[17] On the civilian side, the International Staff (IS) in Brussels accommodated the Intelligence Unit (IU), founded in 2011 following a request from the SG. In principle, IU reported to the NAC and in copy to the Civilian Intelligence Committee (CIC), the body of NATO's national civilian or hybrid intelligence and security services, responsible for matters of espionage and terrorist or related threat.[18] In its day-to-day work, it was supported by the NATO Office of Security (NOS), IS' counterintelligence agency, which advised the SG and the Security Committee (SC) on security concerns and policy matters.[19]

The Intelligence Division (INT) of the International Military Staff (IMS), known as IMS-INT, reported to the MC and in copy to the Military Intelligence Committee (MIC), the Alliance's military CIC equivalent. The civilian IU and the military IMS-INT would both draft non-agreed intelligence reports on a daily basis, including strategic foresight, and provide intelligence support to all NATO HQ elements, NATO Member States and NATO Commands. IMS-INT also exclusively provided NATO-agreed strategic early warning and situational awareness – the so-called NATO Intelligence Warning System

---

[16] Claudia Bernasconi, "NATO's Fight Against Terrorism. Where Do We Stand?", *NATO Defense College Research Paper,* no. 66 (April 2011), 5; Adriana N. Seagle, "Intelligence Sharing Practices Within NATO: An English School Perspective", *International Journal of Intelligence and CounterIntelligence* 28, no. 3 (2015), pp. 559-560.

[17] "Istanbul Summit Communiqué", 28 June 2004.

[18] "Civilian Intelligence Committee (CIC)". *NATO.* Accessed 15 May 2017. http://www.nato.int/cps/en/natolive/topics_69278.htm

[19] "Todd J. Brown. Director NATO Office of Security". *NATO.* Accessed 14 May 2017. http://www.nato.int/cps/en/natohq/who_is_who_112175.htm

(NIWS) – and situational awareness – General Intelligence Estimate (NSIE) or MC-161 series – to all NATO HQ entities and nations.[20]

The global terrorist threat and the Alliance's engagement in CT-inspired military missions resulted in the growing importance within NATO of intelligence sharing on terrorism. As a consequence, in 2003 the Terrorist Threat Intelligence Unit (TTIU) was created at HQ,[21] followed by the joint IS/IMS Intelligence Liaison Unit (ILU) for the exchange of information with non-NATO partners.[22] In 2010, the NAC agreed to establish the Emerging Security Challenges Division (ESCD); ESCD was intended to address a growing range of non-traditional risks and challenges, focusing on CT, cyber defense, Weapons of Mass Destruction (WMD) and energy security.[23] In the process, ESCD's Strategic Analysis Capability (SAC), drafting reports based on open source, diplomatic reports and intelligence, evolved into another HQ assessment asset. SAC, with cyber and so-called science-for-peace as its main priorities, also risked overlap with IMS-INT's NIWS, NATO's early warning tool for (un)known unknowns.

---

[20] "International Military Staff". *NATO*. Accessed 14 May 2017. http://www.nato.int/cps/en/natohq/topics_64557.htm

[21] TTIU was in 2011 absorbed by IS' IU; ILU in 2016 by JISD.

[22] John Kriendler, *NATO Intelligence and Early Warning, Conflict Studies Research Center, Special Series 06/13* (Swindon: Conflict Studies Research Center, 2006), 2; Friedrich W. Korkisch, *NATO Gets Better Intelligence: New Challenges Require New Answers to Satisfy Intelligence Needs for Headquarters and Deployed/Employed Forces* (Vienna: IAS, 2010), 31; Bernasconi, "NATO's Fight Against Terrorism", 3; Seagle, "Intelligence Sharing Practices", p. 569.

[23] Bernasconi, "NATO's Fight Against Terrorism", 3; Brian R. Foster, *Enhancing the Efficiency of NATO Intelligence Under an ASG-I* (Carlisle: United States Army War College, 2013), p. 5.

NATO's intelligence future

On 12 April 2017, the importance of the new position of the ASG-I&S was illustrated when Freytag von Loringhoven was the only ASG to join the SG on his first visit to US President Donald Trump. However, although NATO's intelligence chief is an influential person within the Alliance, his Deputy, US Brig Gen Paul Nelson, told him upon arrival that he would have access to NATO releasable information only and not to all US intelligence.[24]

Intelligence is the first line of defense and therefore instrumental in making the Alliance and its Member States more resilient. The ASG-I&S will need to address the future structure, sharing procedures and content of NATO intelligence. This section of the paper deals with the ASG-I&S' priorities and his do's and don'ts.

Structure

The ASG-I&S has already started to transform NATO's HQ intelligence structure into the new Joint Intelligence and Security Division (JISD). In April 2017, the Assistant Secretary General on Emerging Security Challenges (ASG-ESC), Amb Sorin Ducaru, applauded the ASG-I&S for merging military and civilian intelligence into the JISD. While the implementation of the new unit is still a work in progress, he observed that IU and IMS-INT no longer distributed the same reports, but that fused intelligence was now being received. Ducaru added that to avoid duplication programs and themes were being closely coordinated between ESCD/SAC and JISD and that from his perspective as a consumer, positive results were visible.[25] However, the incorporation of SAC into JISD remains a logical next step, as this would enrich the ASG-I&S' intelligence and early warning products, as well as further excluding duplication of activities.

Within the JISD the merger has resulted in a clash between the civilian and military intelligence pillars.[26] Although this is a normal reaction to an interagency fusion process due to cultural differences, a

---

[24] Meeting with a senior NATO staff member, Brussels, 3 May 2017.

[25] Meeting with ASG-ESC, Amb Sorin Ducaru (ROU), Rome, 7 April 2017.

[26] Meeting with a senior NATO staff member, Brussels, 3 May 2017.

fundamental discussion about security continues to challenge the ASG-I&S. The bottom line is that representatives of CIC/IU adhere to the 'need to know' principle, whereas exponents of MIC/IMS-INT favor the 'need to share' approach. "It is confidence building between two entities that have different strings of DNA", according to a senior staff member.[27] Some of CIC's national civilian services find it unacceptable that the military are sharing intelligence on the Baltic region with non-NATO members Sweden and Finland, whereas the military from an operational perspective view this cooperation as justified and necessary. Some services within CIC are not convinced that the temporary integration of the counterintelligence agency into JISD should obtain permanent status. Even though the new division is made up of an Intelligence Branch and a Security Branch, it is contended that its unique features would not be sufficiently preserved and thus NOS should once more be independent and report to CIC.

The first priority for Freytag von Loringhoven, therefore, should be the implementation of the merger of all intelligence elements at HQ level into an effective JISD. In order to be efficient, the ASG-I&S should be given the mandate to coordinate all intelligence activities at HQ level to avoid any duplication of NATO's scarce capabilities. Currently, at least three agencies at NATO HQ are more or less involved in strategic foresight, and the same three also deal with aspects of strategic early warning. As discussed earlier, a merger of JISD, NOS and ESCD/SAC, the three duplicating agencies identified, not only seems a logical one but should be implemented without further delay. The less preferred option is the continuation of SAC as an analyzing entity without the use of intelligence – making it a paper tiger – whereas the renewed separation of NOS would resurrect the two intelligence pillars and breed discord.

Sharing

To be successful, the ASG-I&S should not try to convince Member States to start sharing sensitive, classified intelligence. Being himself a former Deputy of the BND, he will know that Member States and their national intelligence and security services are by nature reluctant

---

[27] Meeting with a senior NATO staff member, Brussels, 2 May 2017.

to share secrets within NATO. Jennifer Sims already predicted the outcome of such pressure; "If "jointness" [in intelligence] is driven more by political necessity than collection requirements, liaison will tend to be heavily defensive in posture, implicitly adversarial, and therefore hollow, despite political and military leaders' contrary expectations".[28] For instance, although France is likely to cooperate on intelligence if strategic interest is shared and if mutual boots are on the ground,[29] it remains unsympathetic to integration and cooperation within any multilateral environment. A senior official of the French Ministry of Foreign Affairs explained that France would always want to preserve its strategic autonomy.[30]

In sum, the second priority for the ASG-I&S should be accepting the continuation of bilateral arrangements between NATO and its Member States.

Notwithstanding the prominent position of major European nations, the ASG-I&S as his third priority should acknowledge a dominant role for the United States. The United States is not only the Member with the most (operational) intelligence to share, but it will also be crucial in facilitating the (future) technological infrastructure to enable the exchange process.

As his fourth priority, the ASG-I&S should develop sharing as a process, slowly bridging the gap between bilateral, case-by-case liaison and structured multilateral intelligence sharing. As already discussed above, he should continue to accept existing bilateral and multilateral cooperation within the Alliance. Coalitions of the willing, able, likeminded and trusted should be allowed, based on NATO's core tasks, to form communities of interest and start an association process respecting 'need to know, need to share' and excluding 'nice to know'. Chris Clough warned, "Alliances and coalitions have traditionally

---

[28] Jennifer E. Sims, "Foreign Intelligence Liaison: Devils, Deals, and Details", *International Journal of Intelligence and CounterIntelligence* 19, no. 2 (2006), p. 202.

[29] Mahoney Kennan et al., *NATO Intelligence Sharing in the 21st Century. Capstone Research Project* (New York: Columbia School of International and Public Affairs, 2013), p. 3.

[30] Briefing by Mr Etienne de Gonneville (FRA), French Ministry of Foreign Affairs, Paris, 27 March 2017.

been weak in terms of intelligence: as the number of partners increases, so the level of guaranteed security decreases".[31] Although these topic- and mission-oriented coalitions would still depend on the willingness of individual Member States to share intelligence, the chances of successful cooperation would increase because it is easier for a few Allies to collaborate and find common ground than for NATO as a whole.

Content

Absence of a clear and present danger results in national secrets not being shared with NATO, while a rapidly changing world with wicked and immediate problems necessitates improved early warning to enhance resilience. Confronted with non-state actors and (un)known unknowns such as nanotechnologies, cybernetic organisms, biological agents and energy security, timeliness and 'jointness' is essential. Therefore, Freytag von Loringhoven should further develop open source capability within NATO and invest in social media analysis and exploitation.[32] As Lt Gen Samuel Wilson, former Director of the Defense Intelligence Agency (DIA), stated, "Ninety percent of intelligence comes from open sources. [...] The real intelligence hero is Sherlock Holmes, not James Bond".[33]

Fusion of open source and social media analysis with existing intelligence from other disciplines guarantees all-source available products. This should be the ASG-I&S' fifth priority and is especially relevant for strategic foresight and early warning and thus resilience.

Ultimately, success or failure of the ASG-I&S is subject to the relevance of his intelligence products to the consumers. Lars Nicander

---

[31] Clough, "Quid Pro Quo", p. 612.

[32] For open source see: Lars D. Nicander, "Understanding Intelligence Community Innovation in the Post-9/11 World", *International Journal of Intelligence and CounterIntelligence* 24, no. 3 (2011), pp. 546-551. Social media in: Marcos Degaut, "Spies and Policymakers: Intelligence in the Information Age", *Intelligence and National Security* 31, no. 4 (2016), pp. 516-517.

[33] As cited in: Major General Michael T. Flynn, Capt Matt Pottinger and Paul D. Batchelor, *Fixing Intel: A Blueprint for Making Intelligence Relevant in Afghanistan* (Washington, DC: Center for a New American Security, January 2010), p. 23.

wrote, "Intelligence is only as good as the value assigned to it by the users".[34] Similarly, Björn Fägersten called for more interaction between policymakers and intelligence analysts, while pointing out that "[in the end] effective intelligence support is dependent on the clear vision of what is to be supported".[35] Close(r) interaction with the consumers of intelligence – as long as non-politicized intelligence is the outcome – will improve the perception of timeliness, accuracy and reliability (reputation), as well as the weighing of the ready availability, ease and flexibility of use and comprehensiveness (precision) of the products.[36] Therefore, the ASG-I&S' sixth priority should be to build bridges between consumers and producers, starting with the coordination and interpretation of the former's requirements.

Conclusion

Do NATO Member States trust each other enough to cooperate on intelligence and do the national intelligence and security services trust their Alliance and its new intelligence chief to successfully manage the sharing of intelligence? Richard Aldrich was skeptical, "States will happily place some of their military forces under allied command, but hesitate to act similarly in the area of intelligence, where coordination rather than control is the most they will accept".[37] Multinational intelligence cooperation will always be characterized by issues such as lack of a common threat perception, national interest, culture and (political dis)trust and consequently, national services are unlikely to share with NATO as a whole and prefer bilateral arrangements. Any Member State is first a state and then a member. NATO, without a clear

---

[34] Nicander, "Understanding Intelligence Community Innovation", p. 542.

[35] Björn Fägersten, "Forward Resilience in the Age of Hybrid Threats: The Role of European Intelligence", in *Forward Resilience. Protecting Society in an Interconnected World*, ed. Daniel S. Hamilton (Baltimore: Johns Hopkins University, 2014), 124-125. Quote in: Björn Fägersten, "Intelligence and decision-making within the Common Foreign and Security Policy", *Swedish Institute for European Policy Studies* 22 (October 2015), p. 11.

[36] Based on the list by Teitelbaun (2004). As cited in: Degaut, "Spies and Policymakers", pp. 524-525.

[37] Aldrich, "Transatlantic Intelligence and Security Cooperation", p. 737.

and present danger, will not witness structured and transparent intelligence sharing; open source exchange being the exception.

To be successful, the ASG-I&S will have to continuously address the future structure, sharing and content of NATO intelligence. His main focus should be on structure and strive to (1) merge all intelligence entities at HQ level into JISD, removing discord and duplication.

In order to succeed with regards to sharing, the ASG I&S should (2) accept the continuation of bilateral arrangements between NATO and its Member States, without pressuring nations into sharing secrets. In doing so, he should (3) acknowledge the lead nation role for the United States on intelligence and its infrastructure. Simultaneously, but incrementally, the ASG-I&S should (4) invest in bridging the gap between bilateral, case-by-case liaison and structured multilateral sharing, by allowing coalitions of the willing, able, likeminded and trusted to form (topic- or mission-oriented) communities of interest.

Content-wise, he should (5) promote the use of fused open source and social media analysis for strategic foresight and early warning purposes thus enhancing resilience. Ultimately, the success or failure of the ASG-I&S depends on his added value, so he should (6) strive to provide intelligence products relevant to the consumers.

Intelligence is the Alliance's first line of defense for all three of NATO's core tasks. Confronted with (un)known unknowns, improved intelligence sharing allows NATO to be more resilient and enables the Alliance to identify at least some unknowns. Consequently, if the ASG-I&S observes the six recommended priorities, he should receive the outright support of all national intelligence and security services of the Member States, as well as NATO's independent intelligence bodies CIC and MIC. This will allow him to strengthen and optimize the Alliance's intelligence collection, analysis and dissemination process. If thus supported, the ASG-I&S could set the stage for a future where, if the right conditions prevail, more secret intelligence will be shared within the Alliance.

Bibliography

Aldrich, Richard J. "British Intelligence and the Anglo-American 'Special Relationship' during the Cold War," *Review of International Studies* 24, no. 1 (March 1998): 331-351.

Aldrich, Richard J. "Transatlantic Intelligence and Security Cooperation". *International Affairs* 80, no. 4 (2004): 731-753.

Ara, Martin J., Thomas Brand and Brage A. Larssen, *Help A Brother Out: A Case Study in Multinational Intelligence Sharing, NATO SOF.* Monterey: Naval Postgraduate School, December 2011.

Barnes, Julian. "NATO Appoints Its First Intelligence Chief". *Wall Street Journal*, 21 October 2016. Accessed 13 May 2017. https://www.wsj.com/articles/nato-appoints-its-first-intelligence-chief-1477070563

Bernasconi, Claudia. "NATO's Fight Against Terrorism. Where Do We Stand?". *NATO Defense College Research Paper*, no. 66 (April 2011): 1-8.

Clough, Chris. "Quid Pro Quo: The Challenges of International Strategic Intelligence Cooperation." *International Journal of Intelligence and CounterIntelligence* 17, no. 4 (2004): 601-613.

Degaut, Marcos. "Spies and Policymakers: Intelligence in the Information Age". *Intelligence and National Security* 31, no. 4 (2016): 509-531.

Den Boer, Monica. "Counter-Terrorism, Security and Intelligence in the EU: Governance Challenges for Collection, Exchange and Analysis". *Intelligence and National Security* 30, no. 2-3 (2015): 402-419.

Deni, John R. "Beyond Information Sharing: NATO and the Foreign Fighter Threat". *Parameters* 45, no. 2 (Summer 2015): 47-60.

"Deutscher wird erster Geheimdienst-Chef der NATO". *RP Online*. 21 October 2016, Accessed 13 May 2017. http://www.rp-online.de/politik/ausland/deutscher-arndt-freytag-von-loringhoven-wird-erster-geheimdienst-chef-der-nato-aid-1.6342986

Duke, Simon. "Intelligence, security and information flows in CFSP". *Intelligence and National Security* 21, no. 4 (2006): 604-630.

"Ex-BND-Vize übernimmt Geheimdienstposten bei NATO". *n-tv.* 24 October 2016, Accessed 13 May 2017. http://www.n-tv.de/ticker/Ex-BND-Vize-uebernimmt-Geheimdienstposten-bei-Nato-article18921376.html

Fägersten, Björn. "Forward Resilience in the Age of Hybrid Threats: The Role of European Intelligence". In *Forward Resilience. Protecting Society in an Interconnected World.* Edited by Daniel S. Hamilton. Baltimore: Johns Hopkins University, 2015: 113-125.

Fägersten, Björn. "Intelligence and decision-making within the Common Foreign and Security Policy". *Swedish Institute for European Policy Studies* 22 (October 2015): 1-12.

Fägersten, Björn. "For EU eyes only? Intelligence and European security". *European Union Institute for Security Studies,* Brief no. 8 (March 2016): 1-4.

Flynn, Major General Michael T., Capt Matt Pottinger and Paul D. Batchelor. *Fixing Intel: A Blueprint for Making Intelligence Relevant in Afghanistan.* Washington, DC: Center for a New American Security, January 2010.

Foster, Brian R. *Enhancing the Efficiency of NATO Intelligence Under an ASG-I.* Carlisle: United States Army War College, 2013.

"International Military Staff". *NATO.* Accessed 14 May 2017. http://www.nato.int/cps/en/natohq/topics_64557.htm

"Istanbul Summit Communiqué Issued by the Heads of State and Government of the North Atlantic Council, Press Release (2004)096, 28 June 2004". *NATO.* Accessed 13 May 2017. http://www.nato.int/docu/pr/2004/p04-096e.htm

Kennan, Mahoney, Nemanja Mladenovic, Salvador Molina, Adam Scher, Selma Stern and Christopher Zoia. *NATO Intelligence Sharing in the 21st Century. Capstone Research Project.* New York: Columbia School of International and Public Affairs, 2013.

Korkisch, Friedrich W. *NATO Gets Better Intelligence: New Challenges Require New Answers to Satisfy Intelligence Needs for Headquarters and Deployed/Employed Forces.* Vienna: IAS, 2010.

Kriendler, John. *NATO Intelligence and Early Warning, Conflict Studies Research Center, Special Series 06/13.* Swindon: Conflict Studies Research Center, 2006.

Lefebvre, Stéphane. "The Difficulties and Dilemmas of International Intelligence Cooperation". *International Journal of Intelligence and CounterIntelligence* 16, no. 4 (2003): 527-542.

Munton, Don and Karima Fredj. "Sharing Secrets: A Game Theoretic Analysis of International Intelligence Cooperation". *International Journal of Intelligence and CounterIntelligence* 26, no. 4 (2013): 666-692.

Nicander, Lars D. "Understanding Intelligence Community Innovation in the Post-9/11 World". *International Journal of Intelligence and CounterIntelligence* 24, no. 3 (2011): 534-568.

"Prague Summit Declaration Issued by the Heads of State and Government of the North Atlantic Council in Prague on 21 November 2002". *NATO*. Accessed 13 May 2017. http://www.nato.int/docu/pr/2002/p02-127e.htm

Pronk, Daniel G. "Sharing the Burden, Sharing the Secrets. The Fulcrum of Transatlantic Intelligence Cooperation", draft for Conference "Creating and Challenging the Transatlantic Intelligence Community" presented at Woodrow Wilson International Center for Scholars, 30 March-1 April 2017: 1-9.

Reveron, Derek S. "Old Allies, New Friends: Intelligence Sharing in the War of Terror". *Orbis* 50, no. 3 (Summer 2006): 453-468.

Seagle, Adriana N. "Intelligence Sharing Practices Within NATO: An English School Perspective". *International Journal of Intelligence and CounterIntelligence* 28, no. 3 (2015): 557-577.

Shea, Jamie. "Resilience: a core element of collective defence". *NATO Review Magazine*, 2016. Accessed 13 May 2017. http://www.nato.int/docu/review/2016/Also-in-2016/nato-defence-cyber-resilience/EN/index.htm

Sims, Jennifer E. "Foreign Intelligence Liaison: Devils, Deals, and Details". *International Journal of Intelligence and CounterIntelligence* 19, no. 2 (2006): 195-217.

Svendsen, Adam. "The globalization of intelligence since 9/11: Frameworks and operational parameters". *Cambridge Review of International Affairs* 21, no. 1 (2008): 129-144.

Svendsen, Adam D.M. *Intelligence Cooperation and the War on Terror: Anglo-American Security Relations After 9/11*. London and New York: Routledge, 2010.

"Todd J. Brown. Director NATO Office of Security". *NATO.* Accessed 14 May 2017.

http://www.nato.int/cps/en/natohq/who_is_who_112175.htm

Walsh, James Igoe. *The International Politics of Intelligence Sharing.* New York: Columbia University Press, 2009.

Walsh, Patrick F. and Seumas Miller. "Rethinking 'Five Eyes' Security Intelligence Collection Policies and Practice Post Snowden". *Intelligence and National Security* 31, no. 3 (2016): 345-368.

"Warsaw Summit Communiqué Issued by the Heads of State and Government participating in the meeting of the North Atlantic Council in Warsaw 8-9 July 2016, 09 Jul. 2016, Press Release (2016) 100". *NATO.* Accessed 13 May 2017.

http://www.nato.int/cps/en/natohq/official_texts_133169.htm

Wiebes, Cees. "De problemen rond de internationale intelligence liaison". *Justitiële Verkenningen* 30, no. 3 (2004): 70-82.

Wippl, Joseph W. "Intelligence Exchange Through InterIntel". *International Journal of Intelligence and CounterIntelligence* 25, no. 11 (2012): 1-18.

Caroline Linzenmeier

A "Resilient" Strategic Communication – Enhancing the Alliance's Resilience by a strong and coherent Collective Voice

> *"A lie can get halfway around the world before the truth can even get its boots on."* (Mark Twain).

Introduction

Strategic communication is not the Holy Grail[1] to deal with Russian information warfare, whose aims include undermining trust in national governments, therefore affecting the societal dimension of national resilience. However, to enhance both national and the Alliance resilience, Russia's (mis-)use of the media must be dispelled by an increased cohesive strategic communication on both the member states' and the Alliance's levels.

National resilience depends not only on *"infrastructural"* security domains (e.g. resilient energy supplies, resilient food and water resources, ability to cope with mass casualties[2]), but also on societal security aspects, like assured continuity of government and critical government services.[3] Enhancing "societal" resilience to better withstand attack or to recover from such, citizens' trust in and support of their respective national governments is core.

---

[1] Daniel Gage, "The continuing evolution of Strategic Communication within NATO", *The Three Swords Magazine,* 27/2014, p. 55, http://www.jwc.nato.int/images/stories/threeswords/IMPLEMENTING_STRATCOM.pdf

[2] Jamie Shea, "Resilience a Core Element of Collective Defense", *NATO Review,* 2016, http://www.nato.int/docu/Review/2016/Also-in-2016/nato-defence-cyber-resilience/EN/index.htm

[3] Ibid.

Infrastructural and Societal Aspects of Resilience

In the light of the current security environment, a general need for resilience now seems universally accepted within the NATO member states. There still is no commonly agreed definition about "resilience" and there are great differences the way it is applied. Nevertheless, the dimensions and the extent of resilience that have to be reached primarily at national level remain at the top of NATO's agenda because of its correlation with the Alliance's resilience as stated by the Heads of State and Government at the 2016 Warsaw Summit: "Today we have made a commitment to continue to enhance our resilience (…) Civil preparedness is a central pillar of Allies' resilience and a critical enabler for Alliance collective defense.(…)".[4] Thus, efforts to achieve a more coherent understanding of, as well as meet baseline requirements for, resilience are underway in NATO and in the EU.[5]

Likewise, the notion of resilience generates concern with assured continuity of government and critical government services[6] before, during and after an attack. This inevitably refers to the "societal dimension" of a nation: Nations can only deter, survive or recover from an attack when the government and its critical administration institutions and bodies can do so as well.

Societal Resilience and the Human Factor

Societal resilience demands "effective government" before, during and after an attack. Along with the above mentioned "hard" factors of resilience, effective governmental action in democracies is based upon citizens' (voters') trust and support.

---

[4] "Warsaw Summit Communiqué Para 73", NATO 2016. Accessed 29 March 2017, http://www.nato.int/cps/en/natohq/official_texts_133169.htm
[5] General overview in "Forward Resilience: Protecting Society in an Interconnected World, Executive Summary and Menu of Recommendations - Draft for Discussion", ed. Daniel S. Hamilton, Centre for Transatlantic Relation, 2016, p. 1, http://transatlanticrelations.org/wp-content/uploads/2016/12/resilience-forward-book-ex-sum-draft-b.pdf
[6] Shea, "Resilience".

This goes back to the basic expectation of the citizens that "their government protects them" (from terrorism and hybrid threats).[7] The "increased security demand by European citizens"[8] not only shows a lack of political persuasiveness, but also indicates a loss of citizens' trust and support in their governments ("human factor"). Depending on the degree, this loss may pose a threat to domestic social cohesion and hamper effective governmental action.

However, methods of undermining trust in governments and their ability to protect their citizens (this is the aim of propaganda) are nothing new (WWII, Cold War etc.). Even current election campaigns in the US, France and Germany reveal those mechanisms: Playing with citizens' fear of being left alone, discussing an obsolete alliance or the challenges of handling mass migration and terrorist attacks. Even the political opposition's doubt over the government's ability to protect the well-being of its citizens and the nation's prosperity may cause the level of trust in governmental protection to decrease.

In "peacetime", comprehensive public trust in, and support of, governments may arguably be negligible. But faced with the current global security situation with its cross-national and non-linear challenges and threats, e.g. the rise of terrorist groups like ISIS, the tensions between West and East about Crimea or economic decline, it is not an option to neglect public opinion. In addition, it is out of the question to deny people's concern for the current security situation by "treating people like children"[9] or to refuse to tell the whole truth because "a part of these answers could frighten the public".[10] Current domestic political activities on both sides of the Atlantic show the negative effects of governments' negligence in this respect. To this effect

---

[7] Gabor Iklody, Director Crisis Management and Planning Directorate, EEAS, during NDC Senior Course 130, 14 March 2017.
[8] Italian military official under Chatham House Rules during NDC Senior Course 130.
[9] Academic under Chatham House Rules during NDC Senior Course 130.
[10] German Minster of the Interior at a press conference on terrorist attacks in Hannover, Germany, 17 November 2015,
http://www.sport1.de/fussball/dfb-team/2015/11/innenminister-thomas-de-maiziere-aeussert-sich-zu-laenderspiel-absage

"populism is a symptom, it's often the consequence of governments' failure to address issues properly with their citizens".[11]

The Communication Channel as a Source of Irritation

The relation between citizens/public opinion and the government/policy is complex and a significant source of misunderstanding and conflict. Notably so, when the information exchange is mainly channelled through the traditional and social media: press conferences follow every event, parliamentary debates are broadcast live, houndish journalists are always heading for the ultimate story everywhere and anytime.... And never was the public so omniscient of what is going on in the world: everybody writes, posts or comments on something in the virtual world. "The nature of mass communication has changed from being a 'single authority speaking and many listening' to a 'many speak to many' interaction".[12]

Additionally, every transmitting channel is a disruptive factor inherent in itself, either by coincidence, default, lack of quality or knowledge, or by intentional intervention. Information is embedded into a context setting right or wrong, is evaluated, misunderstood or changed, is less fact than opinion, or is just false or fake information. "Whether it is the speed of fake news, politically motivated leaks or hacked information (…): These instruments present a grave challenge to informed public debate."[13] "Today's media landscape (…) is, in many countries increasingly fragmented, polarized, and politicized".[14] "People get

---

[11] Gabor Iklody, Director Crisis Management and Planning Directorate, EEAS during NDC Senior Course 130, 14 March 2017.
[12] Sanda Svetoka, "Social media as a tool of hybrid warfare", *NATO Strategic Communications Centre of Excellence*, ed. Anna Reynolds, Latvia 2016, p. 5, http://www.stratcomcoe.org/social-media-tool-hybrid-warfare
[13] "(Dis)information : Fake It, Leak It, Spread It", in *Munich Security Report (2017)*, https://www.securityconference.de/en/discussion/munich-security-report/munich-security-report-2017/issues/disinformation-fake-it-leak-it-spread-it
[14] Ibid.

different views of the world"[15] and in the worst case, our "Democracies face a fake new world".[16]

Accordingly, the citizens' perception of government actions is shaped through its media coverage.

Advantage: Russia

Russia's information warfare as part of non-linear and cross-national hybrid warfare is going right to the centre of gravity of Western nations by attacking the citizens' trust in assured continuity of government and critical government services, "attacking the European security structure".[17]

Even though there is no universal definition of "hybrid warfare"[18], the various "uses of the media" are always included: "Hybrid warfare is a potent, complex variation of warfare (…) includes traditional and modern media instruments".[19] Using a broad range of activities within hybrid warfare, Russia manages to further its objectives and cast doubt on democratic institutions.[20]

The German "Lisa case"[21], which dominated the headlines and impacted on German public discussion for two weeks in January 2016, serves well as an example: A 13-year-old Russian-German girl in Berlin had gone missing for 30 hours and was reported by the First Rus-

---

[15] Academic under Chatham House Rules during NDC Senior Course 130.
[16] Toomas Hendrick Ilves, "Democracies face a fake new world", in *The World Post by Huffington Post and the Berggruen Institute,* 19 December 2016. Accessed 19.12.2016, http://www.huffingtonpost.com/entry/russia-election-hack_us_5857ebb1e4b08debb789dae6
[17] SHAPE official under Chatham House Rules during NDC Senior Course 130.
[18] Svetoka, "Social media", p. 10.
[19] Ralph D. Thiele, "Building Resilience Readiness against Hybrid Threats - A Cooperative European Union / NATO Perspective", *ISPSW Strategy Series: Focus on Defense and International Security",* No. 449, September 2016, p. 2, http://www.ispsw.com/wp-content/uploads/2016/09/449_Thiele_Malaysia_Sep2016.pdf
[20] "(Dis)information".
[21] Stefan Meister, "The "Lisa case": Germany as a target of Russian disinformation", *NATO Review,* 2016, http://www.nato.int/docu/Review/2016/Also-in-2016/lisa-case-germany-target-russian-disinformation/EN/index.htm

sian TV to have been raped by migrants. The traditional media as well as the social media fora served as multipliers and platforms to mobilize demonstrations and public protest. Furthermore, at the top political level, the Russian Foreign Minister made two public statements about his concerns about the inability of the German police and legal system to take such cases seriously because of political correctness. At the end of the day, the story turned out to be fake (German police were able to confirm that the missing girl had been with a friend), yet was intensively covered by Russian domestic and foreign media, resulting in diplomatic friction between Germany and Russia[22] and eventually escalating into increased social tension and a loss of trust in the current government.

Part of Russia's information warfare is an extensive and a "professional" use of the traditional and the social media, as the "Lisa case" demonstrates all too well: "Implant doubt in public opinion whether they can trust their government, trust in their administration, doubt whether they can defend them".[23]

This "information warfare"[24] is a broad and inclusive concept covering a wide range of different activities: It covers hostile activities using information as a tool, or a target, or a domain of operations.[25] The aims and objectives vary from both "offensive to defensive, from use of as a stand-alone tool for achieving geopolitical goals, to simple weakening of the adversary without necessarily any specific end state in mind."[26] "To this end, they will attempt to influence their target society's collective mind-set so that their values and principles become challenged, their resolve weakened and consequently political objectives are abandoned or modified."[27]

---

[22] Ibid.
[23] Gabor Iklody, Director Crisis Management and Planning Directorate, EEAS, during NDC Senior Course 130, 14 March 2017.
[24] Detailed overview and further recommendations: Keir Giles, "Handbook of Russian Information Warfare", *Fellowship Monograph 9*, November 2016.
[25] Ibid., p. 6.
[26] Ibid., p. 16-17.
[27] Thiele, "Building Resilience", p. 2.

All quiet on the Eastern Front?

Given the vast debates about "hybrid warfare", notable researchers, practitioners as well as military assessments declare: "Hybrid warfare by Russia is nothing new, it's just another nonsense, it's just fighting the war"; [28] "while the topic still is 'something of a novelty that makes it worth studying'".[29]

Technology as well as the development of the media information space feed Russian information warfare. "The hybrid threat changed in its dimensions; there has been propaganda as well before by manipulating news".[30] Russia does not distinguish between several – conventional and modern – forms of warfare. It adapts to the given or developing circumstances and evolves its means and measures based on a traditional Soviet threat assessment where the West continues to pose the threat.[31] Hybrid threats "blur the line between war and peace – combining military aggression with political, diplomatic, economic, cyber and disinformation measures".[32] For example: "Russia's influence in Croatia and the region is made through financing companies and discussing 'alternative' facts in Croatia with the public."[33] Consequently, this information warfare is all-encompassing: "Russia seeks to influence foreign decision-making by supplying polluted information, exploiting the fact, that Western elected represent-

---

[28] Keir Giles, "Russia's 'New' tools for confronting the West - Continuity and Innovation in Moscow's Exercise of Power", *Chatham House Research Paper,* 21 March 2016, p. 3.
https://www.chathamhouse.org/sites/files/chathamhouse/publications/2016-03-russia-new-tools-giles.pdf. British official under Chatham House Rules during NDC Senior Course 130. General (ret) Knud Bartels during NDC Senior Course 130, 4 April 2017.
[29] Keir Giles, "Conclusion: Is Hybrid Warfare Really new?", in *"NATO's Response to hybrid threats",* ed. Guillaume Lasconjarias and Jeffrey A. Larsen, NATO Defense College Forum Paper 24, 2015, p. 321.
[30] NATO official under Chatham House Rules during NDC Senior Course 130.
[31] Giles, "Russia's 'New' tools", p. 2.
[32] German Ministry of Defense, SE I 2, official statement of 13 April 2017.
[33] Drago Keleman, Croatian MoD, Head of Defence Policy Directorate, during NDC Senior Course 130, 31 March 2017.

atives receive and are sensitive to the same information flow as their voters."³⁴

Russia uses every opportunity to manipulate the transmitting medium ("Russian politicians do not hesitate even to lie"³⁵), so as to achieve its objectives: preserving its regime and enhancing its own status as a great power.³⁶ The aim is to control information, in whatever form.³⁷ But still, some may be surprised how rapidly Russia's practice of information warfare has developed.³⁸

It is the dimensions of Russia's information warfare and its constant conduct, not only in "wartime"³⁹ that represent the really dramatic novelty of Russia's information warfare, which should not be underestimated⁴⁰: "The more we leave them opportunities, the more they (the Russians) will take advantage of it."⁴¹ "Perhaps we should rethink our point of view of assessing Russian warfare, not thinking that they are doing warfare as we are doing or thinking it." ⁴²

"Communicating the War is Fighting the War"⁴³

But how to react to this "main threat that citizens' trust in media and politicians further erode, creating a vicious circle that threatens liberal democracy"?⁴⁴ Looking at the "Lisa case", Russia did everything right by quickly entering the scene and emphasizing a piece of "false" information, leading to doubts about the German police. Media coverage and a comment by the Russian Minister of Foreign Affairs led to

---

³⁴ Giles, "Handbook", p. 22.
³⁵ SHAPE official under Chatham House Rules during NDC Senior Course 130.
³⁶ Deborah Yarsike Ball, "Protecting Falsehoods with a Bodyguard of Lies: Putin's Use of Information warfare", *NDC Research Paper no 136,* February 2017, p. 2. http://www.ndc.nato.int/news/news.php?icode=1017
³⁷ Keir Giles, "The next phase of Russian information warfare", Publication of NATO Centre of Excellence, 2017, p. 6,
http://www.stratcomcoe.org/next-phase-russian-information-warfare-keir-giles
³⁸ Giles, "Russia's 'New' tools", p. 8.
³⁹ Ball, "Protecting Falsehoods", p. 9.
⁴⁰ Ibid., p. 16.
⁴¹ NATO official under Chatham House Rules during NDC Senior Course 130.
⁴² SHAPE official under Chatham House Rules during NDC Senior Course 130.
⁴³ Lecturer under Chatham House Rules during NDC Senior Course 130.
⁴⁴ "(Dis)information".

a heated debate about mass migration and the effectiveness of the government.

Despite its complex, opaque propaganda machinery, Russian information warfare follows simple rules: Identify your audience! Identify your message! Identify your channels! And lead the narrative, in the long run and the short! With regard to the aims and objectives of the Russian information warfare (see above), Russia "communicates purposefully to advance its mission."[45] This definition in general terms of strategic communication is also reflected in the Alliance's approach: "NATO Strategic Communications is the coordinated and appropriate use of NATO communications activities and capabilities in support of Alliance policies, operations and activities, and in order to advance NATO's aims."[46]

"Since a primary target for Russian information and disinformation campaigns is mass consciousness, greater public involvement is essential."[47] And Russia dominates the non-linear, cross-national information battle space[48], where "there has been effectively no visible public debate; and this critically undermines those societies' resilience to information attack."[49]

NATO and the member states have to strike back with the means and measures of this battle space: Use a strategic communication respecting legal and ethical standards. Because resilience, for the purpose of "societal security (…) requires not only good crisis management skills,

---

[45] Kirk Hallahan, Derina Holtzhausen, Betteke van Ruler, Dejan Verčič and Krishnamurthy Sriramesh "Defining Strategic Communication". *International Journal of Strategic Communication* (2007), 1: 1, pp. 3-35, p. 4,
https://www.researchgate.net/publication/241730557_Defining_Strategic_Communication

[46] "About Strategic Communication", NATO Strategic Communications Centre of Excellence,
http://www.stratcomcoe.org/about-strategic-communications

[47] Giles, "The next phase", p. 17.

[48] Mari K. Eder, "Leading the Narrative - The Case for Strategic Communication". (Annapolis: Naval Institute Press, 2011), p. 11.

[49] Giles, "The next phase", p. 17.

but also communication effectiveness in both the real and the virtual world".[50]

"Being a member of NATO has benefits but also obligations": national sovereignty and NATO's collective defense commitment. "Both factors together are key to the resilience of the individual nation, giving the citizens trust and confidence and a possible aggressor a clear message, but also resilience of NATO for the same reasons."[51]

Conclusions

Resilience both on national and on Alliance level needs further development (e.g. NATO concept, strategy) and strengthening: both are directly correlated.[52]

To a large extent, resilience is contingent upon societal aspects like assured continuity of governments and their critical administration.

Such societal resilience very much depends on citizens' trust in their governments and their perception of the governments' ability to protect them ("human factor"), which is primarily fostered and channelled by the media.

Russia's information warfare diminishes Western citizens' trust in their governments and in the Alliance by means of disinformation and propaganda.

From this point of view, Russian information warfare is nothing new: It is a "negative" example of strategic communication by exploiting all possibilities of influencing the media and by dominating the "information battle space".

Russia leads the narrative, while the member states as well as NATO show shortfalls in a coherent strategic communication to dispel Russian information warfare, and to promote the member states' and the Alliance's resilience.

---

[50] Marios P. Efthymiopoulos, "NATO Smart Defense and Cyber Resilience", *The Fletcher School - The Constantine Karamanlis Chair,* Working Papers , no. 1 (2016): pp. 37, 22,
http://fletcher.tufts.edu/~/media/Fletcher/Microsites/Karamanlis Chair/PDFs/Karamanlis_WP_May_2016.pdf
[51] German Ministry of Defense, SE I 2, official statement of 13 March 2017.
[52] "Warsaw Summit Communiqué Para 73".

The Warsaw Summit Communiqué and its statement about resilience (see above) omit this human or cognitive dimension[53] by only referring to the "hard"/infrastructural aspects of resilience.

Recommendations

NATO should take the lead to overcome the "political blabla about resilience"[54] as stated at the Warsaw Summit (see above) and gain momentum by "doing the homework".[55]

NATO should address the need to enhance member states' commitment by emphasizing the correlation between NATO's collective defense and mutual benefit (Alliance membership is already a factor for being resilient).

NATO and its member states should strengthen their national and collective understanding and awareness of societal resilience. "Resilience is about predictions and preparing for potential risks",[56] which should incorporate the "human" factor (inform, train, assist) in order to better withstand Russian information warfare/Russia's strategic communication.

NATO should answer "the call for more common action driven by the realization of the scale of the challenge, and respond to the need to join forces and resources"[57] by enhancing the Alliance's analysis competences with regard to any information warfare.

---

[53] Piret Pernik and Tomas Jermalavicius, "Forward Resilience: Protecting Security in an Interconnected World; Resilience as Part of NATO's Strategy: Deterrence by Denial and Cyber Defense"; *Working Paper* of the Centre for Transatlantic Relation, December 2016, p. 1,
http://transatlanticrelations.org/wp-content/uploads/2016/12/Resilience-forward-book-pernik-jermalacivius-final.pdf

[54] Academic under Chatham House Rules during NDC Senior Course 130.

[55] Lorenz Meyer-Minnemann, "Forward Resilience: Protecting Society in an Interconnected World - Resilience and Alliance Security: The Warsaw Commitment to enhance Resilience", *Working Paper* of the Centre for Transatlantic Relation, p. 3,
http://transatlanticrelations.org/wp-content/uploads/2016/12/resilience-forward-book-meyer-minnemann-final.pdf

[56] NATO official under Chatham House Rules during NDC Senior Course 130.

[57] "Forward Resilience -Draft for Discussion", pp. 4-5.

NATO and its member states should immediately develop a coherent and "more robust strategic communication strategy to counter Russia's information operations, particularly where Moscow (…) seek to exploit social and political differences in allied and partner states"[58]. Besides being coherent, this strategic communications approach must be adaptable to national specifics, using the Alliance's assets and national determination: "… analysis dissecting the problem(s), the audience(s), and the message(s), and to be planned and implemented accordingly."[59]

NATO should cooperate more closely with other organizations dealing with resilience and information warfare, like the EU, or the OSCE, by involving and evolving the NATO Strategic Communications Centre of Excellence.[60]

In sum: The Alliance's resilience based upon the resilience of its member states must be enhanced by way of a strong and coherent collective voice: By a "resilient" NATO-coordinated strategic communication.

---

[58] Ibid., (same pages).
[59] "In-depth-analysis - EU strategic communications, With a view to counteracting propaganda", Policy Department of the Directorate-General for External Policies, 2016, pp. 29-30,
http://www.europarl.europa.eu/RegData/etudes/IDAN/2016/578008/EXPO_IDA(2016)578008_EN.pdf
[60] "Forward Resilience - Draft for Discussion", pp. 4-5.

Bibliography

Books

Eder, Mari K. "Leading the Narrative - The Case for Strategic Communication", Annapolis: Naval Institute Press, 2011.

Giles, Keir. "Conclusion: Is Hybrid Warfare Really New?". In *"NATO's Response to hybrid threats"*. Edited by Guillaume Lasconjarias and Jeffrey A. Larsen. NATO Defense College Forum Paper 24, Rome 2015.

Giles, Keir. "Handbook of Russian Information Warfare", *NATO Defense College Fellowship Monograph 9,* Rome, November 2016.

Official Magazines and Research Papers

Ball, Deborah Yarsike. "Protecting Falsehoods with a Bodyguard of Lies: Putin's Use of Information warfare", *NDC Research Paper no 136,* February 2017.
http://www.ndc.nato.int/news/news.php?icode=1017

Efthymiopoulos, Marios P. "NATO Smart Defense and Cyber Resilience", *The Fletcher School - The Constantine Karamanlis Chair,* Working Papers , no. 1 (2016): 37.
http://fletcher.tufts.edu/~/media/Fletcher/Microsites/Karamanlis Chair/PDFs/Karamanlis_WP_May_2016.pdf

Gage, Daniel. "The continuing evolution of Strategic Communication within NATO". *The Three Swords Magazine",* 27/2014, 53-55.
http://www.jwc.nato.int/media/selected-articles-from-the-three-swords-may-2014-issue

Giles, Keir. "Russia's 'New' tools for confronting the West - Continuity and Innovation in Moscow's Exercise of Power". *Chatham House Research Paper,* 21 March 2016.
https://www.chathamhouse.org/sites/files/chathamhouse/publications/2016-03-russia-new-tools-giles.pdf

Giles, Keir. "The next phase of Russian information warfare", Publication of NATO Centre of Excellence, 2017, 17.
http://www.stratcomcoe.org/next-phase-russian-information-warfare-keir-giles

Hallahan, Kirk, Holtzhausen, Derina, van Ruler, Betteke, Verčič, Dejan and Sriramesh, Krishnamurthy. "Defining Strategic Communication". *International Journal of Strategic Communication* (2007), 1: 1, 3-35.

https://www.researchgate.net/publication/241730557_Defining_Strategic_Communication

Ilves, Toomas Hendrick. "Democracies face a fake new world". *The World Post by Huffington Post and the Berggruen Institute,* 19 December 2016, Accessed 19.12.2016.

http://www.huffingtonpost.com/entry/russia-election-hack_us_5857ebb1e4b08debb789dae6

Meister, Stefan. "The "Lisa case": Germany as a target of Russian disinformation", *NATO Review,* 2016.

http://www.nato.int/docu/Review/2016/Also-in-2016/lisa-case-germany-target-russian-disinformation/EN/index.htm

Meyer-Minnemann, Lorenz. "Forward Resilience: Protecting Society in an Interconnected World - Resilience and Alliance Security: The Warsaw Commitment to enhance Resilience". *Working Paper* of the Centre for Transatlantic Relation.

http://transatlanticrelations.org/wp-content/uploads/2016/12/resilience-forward-book-meyer-minnemann-final.pdf

Pernik, Piret and Jermalavicius, Tomas: "Forward Resilience: Protecting Security in an Interconnected World; Resilience as Part of NATO's Strategy: Deterrence by Denial and Cyber Defense". *Working Paper* of the Centre for Transatlantic Relation. December 2016, 1.

http://transatlanticrelations.org/wp-content/uploads/2016/12/Resilience-forward-book-pernik-jermalacivius-final.pdf

Shea, Jamie. "Resilience a Core Element of Collective Defense". *NATO Review,* 2016.

http://www.nato.int/docu/Review/2016/Also-in-2016/nato-defence-cyber-resilience/EN/index.htm

Svetoka, Sanda. "Social media as a tool of hybrid warfare". *NATO Strategic Communications Centre of Excellence*. Edited by Anna Reynolds, Latvia, 2016.

http://www.stratcomcoe.org/social-media-tool-hybrid-warfare

Thiele, Ralph D. "Building Resilience Readiness against Hybrid Threats - A Cooperative European Union / NATO Perspective." *ISPSW Strategy Series: Focus on Defense and International Security"*. No. 449, September 2016.

http://www.ispsw.com/wp-content/uploads/2016/09/449_Thiele_Malaysia_Sep2016.pdf

"(Dis)information: Fake It, Leak It, Spread It". *Munich Security Report (2017)*.

https://www.securityconference.de/en/discussion/munich-security-report/munich-security-report-2017/issues/disinformation-fake-it-leak-it-spread-it

"Forward Resilience: Protecting Society in an Interconnected World, Executive Summary and Menu of Recommendations - Draft for Discussion". Edited by Daniel S. Hamilton. Centre for Transatlantic Relation 2016.

http://transatlanticrelations.org/wp-content/uploads/2016/12/resilience-forward-book-ex-sum-draft-b.pdf

"In-depth-analysis - EU strategic communications, With a view to counteracting propaganda". Policy Department of the Directorate-General for External Policies, 2016.

http://www.europarl.europa.eu/RegData/etudes/IDAN/2016/578008/EXPO_IDA(2016)578008_EN.pdf

Websites

"Warsaw Summit Communiqué". NATO 2016. Accessed 29 March 2017.

http://www.nato.int/cps/en/natohq/official_texts_133169.htm

"About Strategic Communication". NATO Strategic Communications Centre of Excellence.

http://www.stratcomcoe.org/about-strategic-communications

Uwe Hartmann

The Evolution of the Hybrid Threat and Resilience as a Countermeasure[1]

Introduction

The year 2014 marks a strategic 'inflection point' in world history. In order to better understand the new security challenges, NATO officials and member states' governments have used the term of hybrid warfare.[2] Some scholars have criticized it as a buzzword that lacks a clear definition. However, since hybrid warfare is rather about exploiting the vulnerabilities of statecraft than of destroying armed forces, states have slightly different understandings of it according to their specific security challenges. Consequently, for scientific research as well as for security organizations such as NATO, the elaboration of a common definition is not easy and probably not useful.

Drawing conclusions from the analysis of the changed security environment, NATO referred to the concept of resilience. Not surprisingly, this term has also been criticized as meaningless.[3] Apparently, resilience may be better understood if closely related to hybrid warfare as the most significant 'game changer' in security affairs. For that purpose, the question needs to be answered, why states conduct hybrid warfare against NATO and its member states, and what characterizes their strategies. Then, the question on what resilience should focus as a counter measure can be answered.

---

[1] This article was published in a slightly modified version as Research Paper No. 139 of the Research Division of the NATO Defense College in Rome, September 2017.

[2] The scholarly discussion about hybrid warfare is best reflected in Guillaume Lasconjarias and Jeffrey A. Larsen (ed.), *NATO's Response to Hybrid Threats*, (Rome: NATO Defense College, 2015). The historical dimension is reconstructed by Williamson Murray and Peter R. Mansoor, *Hybrid Warfare. Fighting Complex Opponents from the Ancient World to the Present*, (Cambridge: University Press, 2012).

[3] The origins and different understandings of resilience are discussed by Michael Hanisch, "What is Resilience? Ambiguities of a Key Term", *Bundesakademie fuer Sicherheitspolitik, Security Policy Working Paper*, no. 19 (2016).

93

This paper argues that hybrid warfare attacks NATO's strategy-making. It utilizes relative advantages in elaborating, implementing and adjusting strategies that are designed to undermine the statecraft of competing nations and/or the political resolve within security organizations. Since hybrid threats will likely become even more complex and, therefore, unpredictable, NATO and all member states should strengthen their efforts to enhance resilience, particularly in strategy-making. NATO has not grasped this dimension of resilience yet. So far, the Alliance has been focusing rather on technical aspects of resilience as a way of enabling rapid military operations. Consequently, resilience should become the guiding principle of NATO's forthcoming strategic concept.

The Objective of Hybrid Warfare

In broad terms, hybrid warfare can be understood as a creative combination of civil and military ways and means that are deployed in a synchronized manner.[4] The political aim of state or non-state actors that conduct hybrid warfare is to preserve or create non-democratic regimes and increase strategic options to enhance their power in international relations.

Russia serves as an excellent example to support this understanding of hybrid warfare. This country does not possess sufficient resources to win a conventional war against NATO. Consequently, civil means must come to the forefront to the greatest extent possible. Thus, a

---

[4] The novelty of modern hybrid warfare is discussed by Frank G. Hoffman, "Conflict in the 21st Century: The Rise of Hybrid Wars", *Potomac Institute for Policy Studies Arlington*, Virginia (December 2007); Alex Deep, "Hybrid War: Old Concepts, New Techniques", *Small Wars Journal*, 2 March 2015.
https://www.smallwarsjournal.com/print/22276 (Accessed 22 April 2017).

strategy to compete with the West necessarily becomes hybrid and, finally, a "grand strategy".⁵

Conducting hybrid warfare in Ukraine, the Russian government deviates from adhering to the rules of the international system that has not provided 'relative advantages' to Russia.⁶ It is Russia's strong intent to undermine the world order, in particular the European security system, as established after World War II and reinforced after the collapse of the Soviet Union. One way of achieving this aim has been to blur the binary distinction of those terms on which the international system and, in particular, international law is founded: war and peace, state war and civil war, symmetric and asymmetric warfare,

---

⁵ The term 'grand strategy' goes back to the British strategic thinker Basil Liddell Hart (Basil Liddell Hart, *Strategy*, New York: Penguin Books, 1991, pp. 319-333). The Russian strategic thought is analyzed by Stephen R. Covington, "The Culture of Strategic Thought Behind Russia's Modern Approaches to Warfare", *Harvard Kennedy School/Belfer Center for Science and International Affairs*, Paper October 2016; and by Timothy L. Thomas, "Russia Military Strategy", *Foreign Military Studies Office (FMSO)*, Fort Leavenworth/Ks., 2015. In the Russian view, imposing hybrid threats on competing states and organizations is closely connected with enhancing its own resiliency. Realizing that colored revolutions inspired by western values or even triggered by western agents are a threat to the survival of its regime, the Russian government has been implementing a mixture of different ways and means to increase the resilience of its politics, society, and military. Among them are emphasizing the specific Russian culture and fostering nationalism, establishing the West as the enemy of Russia, enhancing the reputation and relevance of the Russian military, establishing a unified command, exercising the military, the people and the government at the same time, and creating frozen conflicts in its near abroad to establish buffer zones. See Christina Varriale, "Rethinking Deterrence and Assurance: Russia's Strategy Relating to Regional Coercion and War, and NATO's Response", *NDC Conference Report* 03/16, October 2016; Covington, "The Culture of Strategic Thought Behind Russia's Modern Approaches to Warfare", p. 23-24; Giles, Keir, Conclusion: "Is Hybrid Warfare Really New?", *NATO's Response to Hybrid Threats*, ed. by Guillaume Lasconjarias and Jeffrey A. Larsen, Rome: NATO Defense College, 2015, pp. 327.

⁶ As John Mearsheimer argues, Russia's revanchist foreign policy must be seen through the lens of Realpolitik, as opposite to the liberal approach to international relations of the West ("Two Worlds, two Playbooks: Why Moscow and Washington don't understand each other", 21.10.2016.).
http://valdaiclub.com/a/higllights/two-worlds-two-playbooks-moscow-and-washington (Accessed 17 April 2017).

combatants and non-combatants are not clear-cut terms any more. Consequently, they have lost their value in analyzing conflicts and in agreeing on how to manage them. In the end, this confusion in language would lead to a world without order and ethos.[7]

Characteristics of the Strategic Approach to Hybrid Warfare

Evidently, bad strategies cannot be healed by tactical or operational successes.[8] Although widely argued that Russia is a declining power, it possesses strength that it utilizes effectively on the strategic level.[9] Its strategic thinking is characterized by the following principles:

- Emphasizing the enemy: Analyze the enemy using scientific methods.[10] The aim is to identify and exploit vulnerabilities of opponents, in particular on the strategic level.
- Developing coherent strategies: Interlink all military (conventional/irregular/nuclear) and civil instruments of statecraft as well as all levels of command (strategic, operational, and tactical) under a

---

[7] Münkler, Herfried, *Kriegssplitter. Die Evolution der Gewalt im 20. und 21. Jahrhundert*, Berlin: Rowohlt, 2015, p. 208; Klaus Naumann, "Europa for alten, neuen und künftigen Gefahren – Herausforderung fuer die Nationen Europas, die EU und die NATO". In: Wolfgang Peischel (Hrsg.), *Wiener Strategie-Konferenz 2016. Strategie neu denken*, Berlin (Miles) 2017, p. 179.

[8] Convincing examples are the "Ostfeldzug" of the German Wehrmacht in World War II and the US war in Vietnam. In spite of significant victories at tactical and operational level, the wars were lost due to failures in strategy-making.

[9] The ends of the Russian strategy are reflected upon in Covington, *The Culture of Strategic Thought behind Russia's Modern Approaches to Warfare*, pp. 41-42, 45; Deborah Yarsike Ball, "Protecting Falshoods: With a Bodyguard of Lies: Putin's Use of Information Warfare", *Research Paper NATO Defense College*, No. 136, Rome February 2017, p. 2 . Ball analyzes the end of regime preservation and the concern of color revolution inspired by the West (pp. 3-7). In this respect, the so-called Gerasimov-doctrine is often referred to. See Charles K. Bartles, "Getting Gerasimov Right", *Military Review*, January/February 2016, pp. 30-38. http://usacac.army.mil/CAC2/MilitaryReview/Archives/English/MilitaryReview_20160228_art009.pdf. (Accessed 24 April 2017).

[10] Bartles, "Getting Gerasimov Right", p. 31. On intelligence see also Sun Tzu, *The Art of War*, translated and with an Introduction by Samuel B. Griffith, London/Oxford/New York: Oxford University Press, 1971.

unified national command that develops, implements, and adjusts the grand strategy.[11]

- Executing strategies ambiguously: Be unpredictable and opportunistic in your actions, and adapt your strategies flexibly to meet unforeseen opportunities and risks.[12]
- Challenging the war paradigm of the West: Refrain from officially declaring and ending wars. Conventional war should be as short as possible[13], while the hybrid threat endures permanently.
- Adhering to the new paradigm of "war among the people"[14]: Instrumentalize the people to act in ways that support your political purposes by e.g. conducting information campaigns, contracting paramilitary forces and utilizing proxies. In Strategic Communication, present Russia as the opposite of the West, thus offering cooperation to all who want to overcome the dominance of the West in the international system. Hit competing states with information campaigns in their territory while controlling the public narrative of its own population.[15]
- Utilizing time as a strategic advantage: Shape the battlefield in advance. Buy time through implementing hidden strategies ('maskirovka') and strategic surprise. Keep the initiative, as West-

---

[11] Covington, *The Culture of Strategic Thought behind Russia's Modern Approaches to Warfare*, pp. 4, 10, 12, 15-16. See also Magarete Klein, "Russia's New Military Doctrine. NATO, the United States and the 'Colour Revolutions'", *SWP-Comments*, No, 9, February 2015.

[12] Covington, *The Culture of Strategic Thought behind Russia's Modern Approaches to Warfare*, pp. 17-20.

[13] See Ralph D. Thiele, "Building Resilience Readiness against Hybrid Threats – A Cooperative European Union / NATO Perspective", *ISPSW Strategy Series: Focus on Defense and International Security*, No. 449, September 2016. http://www.ispsw.com/wp-content/uploads/2016/09/449_Thiele_Malaysia_Sep2016.pdf. (Accessed 10 April 2017). See also Covington, "The Culture of Strategic Thought Behind Russia's Modern Approaches to Warfare", pp. 34, 36-38.

[14] Sir Rupert Smith, *The Utility of Force*, New York: Random House, 2007.

[15] The re-emergence of the importance of controlling narratives and discrediting the West is described in Ball, "Protecting Falshoods", pp. 9-13.

ern states have difficulties in predicting conflicts and conducting preemptive action, as well as in reconstructing hybrid warfare.[16]
- <u>Utilizing the military without risking strategic defeat:</u> Integrate military ways and means to threaten governments and people, to support civil actors, and to protect your own territory against military responses of NATO (e.g. through A2AD, high-precision weapons).[17]

Russia's approach to strategy-making attacks perceived weaknesses of NATO and its member states. In particular, Russia learned from the US and its allies in Afghanistan and Iraq that western states struggle in developing coherent strategies for political (non-existential) conflicts.[18] Countering hybrid threats should, therefore, not focus exclusively on the three Baltic States that see themselves in the middle of a hybrid war with Russia[19]. By contrast, the center of gravity of Russia's hybrid warfare is likely placed on the US and major European nations that drive the strategic decision-making processes in NATO.

---

[16] Covington, *The Culture of Strategic Thought behind Russia's Modern Approaches to Warfare*, pp. 13-20; Bartles, "Getting Gerasimov Right", p. 31

[17] Covington, *The Culture of Strategic Thought behind Russia's Modern Approaches to Warfare*, pp. 29.

[18] One senior US official from the Pentagon underlined, during a lecture at the NDC in Rome, that the Russians "… looked at us and saw us struggling in Afghanistan and Iraq". The difficulties in strategy-making of the US are described by Ricks (Thomas E. Ricks, *Fiasko. The American Military Adventure in Iraq*, London: Penguin Books, 2007) and Woodward (Bob Woodward, *Obama's Wars*, (New York/London/Tokyo/Sydney: Simon &Schuster, 2010). To attack the strategic level of an enemy is one of the principles of the Chinese strategic advisor Sun Tzu. See Baylis, John and Wirtz, James J. and Gray, Colin S., *Strategy in the contemporary World*, New York: Oxford University Press, 2010, p. 78.

[19] Andrew Radin, "Hybrid Warfare in the Baltics. Threats and Potential Responses", *RAND Corporation* 2017. http://www.rand.org/pubs/research_reports/RR1577.html. (Accessed 22 April 2017). The result that the three Baltic states are most endangered by a large-scale conventional attack does not exclude the threat analysis that these states have already been in a hybrid war with Russia. A potential hybrid warfare scenario for the Baltic states is described by Mark Galeotti, "Time to Think About 'Hybrid Defense'", *War on the Rocks*, 30 July 2015. https://warontherocks.com/2015/07/time-to-think-about-hybrid-defense (Accessed 17 April 2017).

Resilience as a Countermeasure

With the rise of hybrid warfare, the scholarly discussion about resilience has related this term to the increasing complexity of the modern security environment, the changing threats and the unpredictability of attacks. Democratic states cannot guarantee complete security without becoming the enemies of their open societies.[20] Consequently, international organizations as well as state institutions, and even individuals, must somehow be prepared to absorb shocks, recover fast in order to conduct counteraction, and learn from it. In the best case, resilience can also contribute to deterring further hybrid attacks.[21]

NATO has decided to enhancing resilience as one of its measures to counter hybrid threats.[22] At the last summit in Warsaw, member states agreed on the significance of nations' commitment to common

---

[20] With respect to complexity and uncertainty, see Jean Boulton, "Embracing Complexity: towards fairness, sustainability and happiness", *openDemocracyUK*, 27 July 2016.
https://www.opendemocracy.net/uk/austerity-media/jean-boulton/embracing-complexity-towards-fairness-sustainability-and-happiness. (Accessed 15 March 2017). Already in 2011, Corinne Bara and Gabriel Broennigmann identified the trend that "facing a variety of different risks – from natural hazards and the failure of critical infrastructures to terrorist attacks – policy-makers have recognized that not all disasters can be averted, and security can never be fully achieved. As a consequence, the focus has shifted from averting, deterring, and protecting from threats to mitigating the consequences should a disaster occur." (Corinne Bara and Gabriel Broennigmann, "Resilience. Trends in Policy and Research", *ETH Zuerich, Center for Security Studies CSS*, April 2011, p. 6.). The threats to democratic societies are analyzed by the philosopher Carl R. Popper in his book *The Open Society and its Enemies*, originally published in 1945 (New Jersey: Princeton University Press, 2013).

[21] Wide agreement exists among scholars on these tasks for resilience. See among others Jamie Shea, "Resilience: a core element of collective defence", *NATO Review Magazine*, p. 4.
http://www.nato.int/docu/Review/2016/Also-in-2016/nato-defence-cyber-resilience/EN/index.htm (Accessed 17 April 2017).

[22] NATO's strategy on countering hybrid threats is a classified document. Articles refer to this strategy, among others "Successful 'Countering Hybrid Threats' experiment in Estonia", *Allied Command Transformation*.
http://www.act.nato.int/successful-countering-hybrid-threats-experiment-in-estonia (accessed 23 April 2017).

values as well as on seven 'baseline requirements'.²³ These requirements reflect a view on resilience that is very much driven by operational demands of collective defense. Progress in these areas is indispensable. However, baseline requirements such as energy, food and water supply or civilian transportation do not provide the necessary resilience in strategy-making where hybrid warfare leverages the weaknesses of NATO. The utility of agile and sustainable conventional forces will be low when the strategy-making processes do not meet the challenges imposed by competitors, and remain an easy target for their hybrid attacks. Therefore, NATO's and its member states' strategy-making processes should be critically analyzed. Resilience should primarily focus on hybrid attacks that are designed to destabilizing functioning alliances and states, polarizing societies, and spreading distrust against the military, and that are most dangerous when they hit the seams where the "fascinating trinity" of the government, the people and the military interact in strategy-making.²⁴

Which principles of strategy-making help to enhance resiliency? And which strengths and weaknesses does NATO have in strategy-making?

- <u>Being self-critical</u>: Honestly and critically reflect upon weaknesses within NATO as an organization, and its member states. Due to its perceived singularity and exceptionality, NATO has been rather critical against others but not so much against itself. Consequently, the biggest threat to NATO is imposed by the member states themselves.²⁵

---

²³ The 'baseline requirements' are described by Lorenz Meyer-Minnemann, "Forward Resilience: Protecting Society in an Interconnected World. Working Paper Series. Resilience and Alliance Security: The Warsaw Commitment to Enhance Resilience", *Johns Hopkins School of Advanced International Studies*, pp. 2-3.

²⁴ Julian Lindley-French, "NATO and New Ways of Warfare: Defeating Hybrid Threats", *NDC Conference Report*, No. 3, Rome May 2015, p. 1. Carl von Clausewitz describes these three stakeholders as a "fascinating trinity" (Carl von Clausewitz, *On War*, edited and translated by Michael Howard and Peter Paret, Princeton/New Jersey: Princeton University Press, 1984, p. 89).

²⁵ As highlighted by a high ranking retired general from NATO HQ during a lecture at the NDC in April 2017: "The biggest threat to NATO is ourselves."

- Understanding strategy-making as a permanent process: Constantly rebalance ends, ways, and means with all stakeholders involved. NATO has established processes that meet some basic requirements of strategy-making as well as the expectations of member states. However, significant disconnects exist: First, even major European nations do not possess institutions designed for strategy-making. Second, cohesion between the processes to generate resources and the conduct of military operations is limited; often, a mismatch exists between ends and means;[26] and nations do not honestly report their actual military capabilities.[27] Third, different strategic cultures exist among NATO member states[28] and also between NATO and other international organizations.
- Respecting all stakeholders involved: Enhance mutual trust to improve synchronization. Civil officials in NATO HQ should not disrespect military personnel nor should the military treat civil partners as "'second-rate citizens' on operations"[29]. Dialogue between politicians and their military advisors remains an "unequal dialogue"[30], since politicians have to decide. However, it is still a dialogue in which military personnel must have the opportunity to

---

[26] Next to missing military capabilities, also political inertia of NATO and its member states must be taken into account. See Lindley-French, "NATO and New Ways of Warfare", p. 1. A representative of Allied Command Operations stated during a visit of the NDC in May 2017 that the link between the planning of capacities and the conduct of operations is broken.

[27] As stated by a high-ranking retired NATO general during a top table lunch at the NDC in April 2017: "If nations want to lie to NATO, they do so."

[28] See *Strategic Cultures in Europe. Security and Defence Policies Across the Continent*, ed. by Heiko Biehl et al., Wiesbaden (Springer) 2013.

[29] Alan Ryan, "The Strategic Civilian: Challenges for Non-Combatants in 21st Century Warfare", *Small Wars Journal*, Journal Article March 31, 2016, p. 9. http://smallwarsjournal.com/jrnl/art/the-strategic-civilian-challenges-for-non-combatants-in-21st-century-warfare (Accessed 12 April 2017).

[30] Elliot A. Cohen, *Supreme Command. Soldiers, Statesmen, and Leadership in Wartime*, (New York: Anchor Books, 2013).

give their best advice. Nations and NATO HQ face significant stress in civil-military relations.³¹

- Involving societies: Overcome the increasing alienation from civilians. The people are important in order to accept, support, and sustain strategies. To enhance their interest in security policy, politicians should address security questions to their electorates, and officials and officers should discuss security issues publicly. Propaganda campaigns that are targeted against specific groups of society should be countered by public diplomacy campaigns based on truth and freedom of media.³² The limited involvement of society seems to be the weakest point in Western strategy-making.

- Arguing about the truth instead of pursuing national interests: Keep the consensus rule within NATO, but clarify its purpose. Consensus prevents defection of member states from decisions, and thus enhances cohesion. However, some nations utilize it as a tool to enforce their national interests, while others try to generate win-win situations. The best way to enhance cohesion, unity of effort, support of the people, and, thus, resilience would be to encourage debate in order to find the best solution beyond national interests.³³

- Educating and selecting the right personnel and emphasizing mission command: Educate leaders who think critically on the strategic level and who thrive in situations of uncertainty.³⁴ Mission command is the leadership philosophy that is most appropriate to

---

[31] Klaus Naumann, *Einsatz ohne Ziel? Zur Politikbedürftigkeit des Militärischen*, Hamburg: Mittelweg, 2006; Hew Strachan, *The Direction of War*, New York: Cambridge University Press, 2013. A representative of Allied Command Operations stated during a visit of the NDC in May 2017: "Politics is the enemy of strategy."

[32] Sven Biscop, "Hybrid Hyseria", *Security Policy Brief*, No. 64 (June 2015), p. 3-4. http://aei.pitt.edu/64790/ (Accessed 20 April 2017).

[33] As an example of the constructivist approach to international relations see Thomas Risse, "Let's argue!: Communicative Action in World Politics", in *International Organization* 54, No. 1, Winter 2000, p. 10.

[34] Critical thinking on strategic levels is discussed by Stephen J. Gerras, "Thinking Critically about Critical Thinking: A Fundamental Guide for Strategic Leaders", *US Army War College*, Carlisle, August 2008.

complexity and uncertainty.[35] Resiliency requires improving educational efforts and linking mission command on tactical and operational level with the strategic level.

- <u>Revitalizing the comprehensive approach</u>: Achieve a better cooperation in spite of divergent organizational interests, limited understanding and different expectations among partners through improved information sharing as well as shared planning and education. The resilience of civil partners, on which the success of military operations depends on, can be increased if the military is capable of complementing their activities and taking over their tasks for a limited period of time, if required.

All these principles of strategy-making are major insights of the scientific community in security policies. Their positive impact on resilience is evident. However, they are not deeply enshrined in NATO's strategic culture. [36] The consequences are severe: Even if NATO had sufficient conventional forces to conduct major operations for collective defense, their utility will remain limited unless the strategy-making processes are significantly improved. [37] The Improvement of NATO's strategy-making through the adaptation of its strategic culture is most decisive for the enhancement of resilience.

---

[35] Ingo Wittmann, *Auftragstaktik. Just a command technique or the core pillar of mastering the military operational art?*, Berlin: Miles, 2012

[36] The concept of strategic culture was designed to challenge the assumptions of many theories of international relations that the state is a rational actor. By contrast, interests and actions are developed in a complex environment of culturally and historically founded beliefs and values within a society that are recognizable and influence foreign policy decisions. See *Strategic Cultures in Europe. Security and Defence Policies Across the Continent*, ed. by Heiko Biehl et al., Wiesbaden: Springer, 2013, pp. 8-12.

[37] This requires more than accelerated decision-making. See "Defence Ministers decide to bolster the Nato Response Force, reinforce Collective Defence", *NATO*, 24 June 2015
 (http://www.nato.int/cps/en/natohq/news_120993.htm) (Accessed 12 April 2017).

The Evolution of Hybrid Threats until 2035

How can competitive or opponent actors use ways and means available within the next 20 years to prevent NATO from accomplishing its mission? Based on a SWOT-analysis[38], specific conclusions can be drawn on how NATO and its member states should enhance their resilience to achieve their political aims. Among the future major challenges not covered in this analysis so far, the people and technology are of utmost importance.

The people

While societies in many Western states have become post-heroic and older[39], states particularly in Africa and the Middle East are challenged by a youth bulge that comes along with extremely high unemployment and, at the same time, empowerment[40]. Competing state and non-state actors are likely to transform the empowerment of unemployed youth in radicalization, including uprisings and terrorism. Mission areas of NATO (e.g. the Balkans and Afghanistan) as well as megacities are ideal locations to create turmoil and chaos, unfreeze frozen conflicts, and, finally, overburden NATO.

Technology

Technological developments will probably contribute to undermining the superiority of western states: by the quicker use of technologies for disruptive tactics and techniques in all domains, including space[41]. Resilience requires faster and better coordinated strategic processes in terms of force planning and acquisition within NATO and its member states.

Significant future threats will make the execution of NATO's mission even more difficult. Next to adapting the cumbersome processes in

---

[38] See Annex A.

[39] Münkler, *Kriegssplitter*, pp. 169-187.

[40] *World Economic Forum, Insight Report: The Global Risks Report 2017*, 12th Edition.

[41] Muresan, Liviu and Georgescu, Alexandru, "The Road to Resilience in 2050. Critical Space Infrastructure and Space Security, *The RUSI Journal*, vol. 160:6 (2015), p. 64.

force planning as a major element of strategy making, the main focus should be placed on the empowerment of the people in NATO member states and also beyond. This includes transparency of strategies, the critical evaluation of past strategies and operations, initiating and sustaining a NATO-wide debate on security related issues, actively seeking the participation of civil society, and initiatives on strategic education of its personnel. Another important area is the 'new approach' to cooperation with international organizations and industry, and particularly with the EU. The EU is not only a major stakeholder in enhancing resilience of those states that belong to both, the EU and NATO. The EU is also a powerful driver in promoting stability and addressing the needs of the youth in Africa and the Middle East. In countering hybrid threats, NATO has become dependent on the EU. [42] This should trigger new attitudes of NATO in its cooperation with the EU that includes common strategic planning.[43]

Conclusion

NATO's history can be written as a sequence of successes but also as a history of internal crises. So far, its impressive record of this form of 'crisis management' has strengthened NATO's adaptability to meet new security requirements.[44] With the evolution of hybrid threats, NATO's core business is at stake: that is strategy-making. Again, NATO must adapt itself.

NATO as an organization but also all member states should enhance resilience with specific emphasis on the strategic level. Those member states that have been driving the decision-making processes in NATO, should take over the leadership. In parallel, the top civil and

---

[42] Also the World Bank (WB) and the International Monetary Fund (IMF) are important stakeholders that can contribute to NATO's mission. During presentations by representatives of both organizations in Washington in May 2017, the clear interest of increased cooperation with NATO with voiced.

[43] NATO may consider to propose an agreement with the EU that is a reversed 'Berlin plus'. Then, NATO would have access to EU civilian capabilities and intelligence.

[44] Uwe Hartmann, *Carl von Clausewitz and the Making of Modern Strategy*, Berlin: Miles 2002, pp. 100-106.

military leadership within NATO should initiate changes in its strategic culture in accordance with the principles as laid down in chapter 4. This process may be inspired by scholars and could even utilize audits by external agencies. It is of utmost importance that the leadership explains the urgency of this adaptation and communicates a clear vision on its intended results.[45] Finally, NATO can utilize its unique strength as a socializing institution to influence the strategic cultures also within its member states.

Understanding resilience beyond the seven baseline requirements is of utmost importance to foster NATO's future relevance. Otherwise, NATO's relevance as an alliance that focuses on the application of military power will be undermined. Consequently, resilience should become the guiding principle for the work on NATO's forthcoming strategic concept. Emphasizing resilience, this concept

- provides a deeper understanding of the complexity of modern warfare;
- indicates that NATO is willing to adapt itself, particularly in its strategy-making;
- sets the main effort on improving interaction between politics, the people and the armed forces;
- counters the "perpetual competition"[46] of hybrid warfare with a permanent adaptation process that has the potential to undermine the utility of hybrid warfare and, thus, deters opponents;
- provides a comprehensive and "… comparative strategic perspective of NATO's southern and eastern flanks, while allowing for a differentiated response"[47];
- allows planning without referring to an adversary such as Russia, "because making a plan constitutes a political decision"[48];

---

[45] John P. Kotter, *Leading Change*, Boston: Harvard Business Review Press 2012.

[46] Philip M. Breedlove, "Foreword", in *NATO's Response to Hybrid Threats*, edited by Guillaume Lasconjarias and Jeffrey A. Larsen, Rome: NATO Defense College, 2015, p. xxii; Nadia Schadlow, "The Problem with Hybrid Warfare", *War on the Rocks*, p. 1.

[47] Andreas Jacobs and Guillaume Lasconjarias, "NATO's Hybrid Flanks. Handling Unconventional Warfare in the South und the East", *Research Paper NATO Defense College*, No. 112, Rome April 2015, p. 12.

- creates a new foundation for equal dialogue and cooperation with international organizations, in particular the EU; and, finally and most importantly,
- increases the utility of NATO's military forces.

Thus, resilience becomes an overarching core theme that spans across the three pillars of NATO's strategic concept and serves as their first line of defense in an increasingly complex security environment.

---

[48] Giles, "Conclusion: Is Hybrid Warfare Really New", p. 325.

Bibliography

Ball, Deborah Yarsike, "Protecting Falshoods: With a Bodyguard of Lies: Putin's Use of Information Warfare", *Research Paper NATO Defense College*, No. 136, Rome February 2017.

Bara, Corinne and Broennigmann, Gabriel, "Resilience. Trends in Policy and Research", *ETH Zuerich, Center for Security Studies CSS*, April 2011.

Bartles, Charles K., "Getting Gerasimov Right", *Military Review*, January/February 2016, pp. 30-38.
http://usacac.army.mil/CAC2/MilitaryReview/Archives/English/MilitaryReview_20160228_art009.pdf.

Baylis, John and Wirtz, James J. and Gray, Colin S., *Strategy in the contemporary World*, New York: Oxford University Press: 2010.

Biehl, Heiko, Giegerich, Bastian, Jonas, Alexandra (ed.), *Strategic Cultures in Europe. Security and Defence Policies Across the Continent*, Wiesbaden: Springer, 2013.

Biscop, Sven, "Hybrid Hyseria", *Security Policy Brief*, No. 64 (June 2015).
http://aei.pitt.edu/64790/

Boulton, Jean, "Embracing Complexity: towards fairness, sustainability and happiness", *openDemocracyUK*, 27 July 2016.
https://www.opendemocracy.net/uk/austerity-media/jean-boulton/embracing-complexity-towards-fairness-sustainability-and-happiness.

Breedlove, Philip M., Forword. In: *NATO's Response to Hybrid Threats*, edited by Guillaume Lasconjarias and Jeffrey A. Larsen, Rome: NATO Defense College, 2015, pp. xxi-xv.

Clausewitz, Carl von, *On War*, edited and translated by Michael Howard and Peter Paret, Princeton/New Jersey: Princeton University Press, 1984

Cohen, Elliot A., *Supreme Command. Soldiers, Statesmen, and Leadership in Wartime*. New York: Anchor Books, 2013.

Covington, Stephen R., "The Culture of Strategic Thought Behind Russia's Modern Approaches to Warfare", *Harvard Kennedy School/Belfer Center for Science and International Affairs*, Paper October 2016.
http://www.belfercenter.org/publication/culture-strategic-thought-behind-russias-modern-approaches-warfare

Deep, Alex, "Hybrid War: Old Concepts, New Techniques", Small Wars Journal, 2 March 2015.
https://www.smallwarsjournal.com/print/22276

"Defence Ministers decide to bolster the Nato Response Force, reinforce Collective Defence", *NATO*, 24 Juni 2015.
http://www.nato.int/cps/en/natohq/news_120993.htm.

Ford, Matthew, Rose, Patrick, Body, Howard, "COIN is Dead – Long Live Transformation", *Parameters. The US Army War College Quarterly*, Vol. XLII, No. 3 (Autumn 2012), pp. 32-43.

Galeotti, Mark, "Time to Think About 'Hybrid Defense'", *War on the Rocks*, 30 July 2015
https://warontherocks.com/2015/07/time-to-think-about-hybrid-defense/

Gerras, Stephen J., "Thinking Critically about Critical Thinking: A Fundamental Guide for Strategic Leaders", *US Army War College*, Carlisle, August 2008.
http://www.au.af.mil/au/awc/awcgate/army-usawc/crit_thkg_gerras.pdf

Giles, Keir, Conclusion: "Is Hybrid Warfare Really New?", *NATO's Response to Hybrid Threats*, ed. by Guillaume Lasconjarias and Jeffrey A. Larsen, Rome: NATO Defense College, 2015, pp. 321-337.

Hanisch, Michael, "What is Resilience? Ambiguities of a Key Term", *Bundesakademie fuer Sicherheitspolitik, Security Policy Working Paper*, no. 19 (2016).
https://www.baks.bund.de/sites/baks010/files/working_paper_2016_19.pdf

Hartmann, Uwe, *Carl von Clausewitz and the Making of Modern Strategy*, Berlin: Miles 2002.

Headquarters Department of the Army, "Hybrid Threats", *Training Circular,* No.7-100, Washington D.C. (26 November 2010).

Hoffman, Frank G., "Conflict in the 21st Century: The Rise of Hybrid Wars", *Potomac Institute for Policy Studies Arlington,* Virginia (December 2007).

Hoffman, Frank G., "Hybrid Warfare and Challenges", *JFH*, issue 52 (1st quarter 2009), pp. 34-39.

Huovinen, Petri, "Hybrid Warfare – Just a Twist of Compound Warfare?", *National Defence University, Department of Military History*, April 2011

https://www.doria.fi/bitstream/handle/10024/74215/E4081_HuovinenKPO_EUK63.pdf.

Jacobs, Andreas and Lasconjarias, Guillaume, "NATO's Hybrid Flanks. Handling Unconventional Warfare in the South und the East", *Research Paper NATO Defense College,* No. 112, Rome (April 2015).

Johnson, David E., "Military Capabilities for Hybrid War. Insights from the Israel defense forces in Lebanon and Gaza", *Occasional Paper RAND Corporation* (2010).

http://www.rand.org/content/dam/rand/pubs/occasional_papers/2010/RAND_OP285.pdf

Klein, Magarete, "Russia's New Military Doctrine. NATO, the United States and the 'Colour Revolutions'", *SWP-Comments*, No. 9, February 2015.

Kotter, John P., *Leading Change,* Boston: Harvard Business Review Press 2012.

Kramer, Franklin D., Binnendijk, Hans, and Daniel S. Hamilton, "NATO's new Strategy: Stability Generation", *Atlantic Council. Brent Scowcroft Center on International Security*, Washington D.C., September 2015.

Lasconjarias, Guillaume and Larsen, Jeffrey A. (ed.), *NATO's Response to Hybrid Threats,* Rome: NATO Defense College, 2015.

Liddell Hart, Basil, *Strategy.* New York: Penguin Books, 1991.

Lindley-French, Julian, "NATO and New Ways of Warfare: Defeating Hybrid Threats", *NDC Conference Report*, No. 3, Rome May 2015.
https://centrostudistrategicicarlodecristoforis.files.wordpress.com/2015/05/jlf-nato-conference-report-190515.pdf

Major, Claudia, "NATO's Strategic Adaptation. Germany is the Backbone for the Alliance's Military Reorganisation", *SWP Comments*, No. 16, Berlin (March 2015).
https://www.swp-berlin.org/fileadmin/contents/products/comments/2015C16_mjr.pdf

Major, Claudia, Moelling, Christian, "A Hybrid Security Policy for Europe", *SWP-Comments*, No. 22, Berlin (April 2015).
https://www.swp-berlin.org/fileadmin/contents/products/comments/2015C22_mjr_mlg.pdf

Mattis, James N. and Hoffmann, Frank, "Future Warfare: The Rise of Hybrid Wars", *U.S. Naval Institute*, Vol. 132/11/1,233 (November 2005).

Meyer-Minnemann, Lorenz, "Forward Resilience: Protecting Society in an Interconnected World. Working Paper Series. Resilience and Alliance Security: The Warsaw Commitment to Enhance Resilience", *Johns Hopkins School of Advanced International Studies*.

Münkler, Herfried, *Kriegssplitter. Die Evolution der Gewalt im 20. und 21. Jahrhundert*, Berlin: Rowohlt, 2015.

Muresan, Liviu and Georgescu, Alexandru, "The Road to Resilience in 2050. Critical Space Infrastructure and Space Security", *The RUSI Journal*, vol. 160:6 (2015), pp. 58-66.

Murray, Williamson and Mansoor, Peter R., *Hybrid Warfare. Fighting Complex Opponents from the Ancient World to the Present*, (Cambridge: University Press, 2012).

Naumann, Klaus, "Europa for alten, neuen und künftigen Gefahren – Herausforderung fuer die Nationen Europas, die EU und die NATO", in *Wiener Strategie-Konferenz 2016. Strategie neu denken*, edited by Wolfgang Peischel, Berlin: Miles, 2017, p. 178-190.

Popper, Carl R., *The Open Society and its Enemies*, New Jersey: Princeton University Press, 2013.

Andrew Radin, "Hybrid Warfare in the Baltics. Threats and Potential Responses", *RAND Corporation* 2017.
http://www.rand.org/pubs/research_reports/RR1577.html

Ricks, Thomas E., *Fiasko. The American Military Adventure in Iraq*, London: Penguin Books, 2007.

Risse, Thomas, "Let's argue!: Communicative Action in World Politics", in *International Organization* 54, No. 1, Winter 2000.

Rumsfeld, Donald, *Known and Unknown. A Memoir*, New York (Penguin Group) 2011.

Ryan, Alan, "The Strategic Civilian: Challenges for Non-Combatants in 21st Century Warfare. Small Wars Journal", *Journal Article* (31 March 2016).

Schadlow, Nadia, "The Problem with Hybrid Warfare", *War on the Rocks*, April 2015.
https://warontherocks.com/2015/04/the-problem-with-hybrid-warfare/

Seselgyte, Margarita, "Can Hybrid War Become the Main security Challenge for Eastern Europe?", *European Leadership Network*, 17 October 2014.
http://www.europeanleadershipnetwork.org/can-hybrid-war-become-the-main-security-challenge-for-eastern-europe_2025.html

Shea, Jamie, "Resilience: a core element of collective defence", *NATO Review Magazine*
http://www.nato.int/docu/Review/2016/Also-in-2016/nato-defence-cyber-resilience/EN/index.htm

Sir Rupert Smith, *The Utility of Force*. New York: Random House, 2007.

Strachan, Hew, *The Direction of War*. New York: Cambridge University Press, 2013.

"Successful 'Countering Hybrid Threats' experiment in Estonia", *Allied Command Transformation*.

http://www.act.nato.int/successful-countering-hybrid-threats-experiment-in-estonia.

Tamminga, Oliver, "Hybride Kriegsführung. Zur Einordnung einer aktuellen Erscheinungsform des Krieges", *SWP-Aktuell*, No. 27, Berlin (Maerz 2015).

https://www.swp-berlin.org/fileadmin/contents/products/aktuell/2015A27_tga.pdf

Thiele, Ralph D., "Building Resilience Readiness against Hybrid Threats – A Cooperative European Union / NATO Perspective", *ISPSW Strategy Series: Focus on Defense and International Security*, No. 449, September 2016.

http://www.ispsw.com/wp-content/uploads/2016/09/449_Thiele_Malaysia_Sep2016.pdf

"Two Worlds, two Playbooks: Why Moscow and Washington don't understand each other", 21.10.2016.

http://valdaiclub.com/a/higllights/two-worlds-two-playbooks-moscow-and-washington.

Varriale, Christina, "Rethinking Deterrence and Assurance: Russia's Strategy Relating to Regional Coercion and War, and NATO's Response", *NDC Conference Report*, 03/16, October 2016.

http://www.ndc.nato.int/news/news.php?icode=984

Wittmann, Ingo, *Auftragstaktik. Just a command technique or the core pillar of mastering the military operational art?* Berlin: Miles, 2012.

Woodward, Bob, *Obama's Wars*. New York/London/Tokyo/Sydney: Simon&Schuster, 2010.

Frank Wasgindt
Smart Power as a relevant Instrument for a future NATO Strategy

Introduction

Soft Power is not a new invention. The resources of Soft Power as the basis for successfully leading a state have existed for hundreds of years. Merely the clear allocation of these resources to power concepts and their definitions is new. The concept of Soft Power was academically stamped by Professor Nye at the beginning of the 1990s. From his perspective at that time the implementation of the power concept has to differentiate between Hard Power (military and economic power) and Soft Power (all other power resources). His concept of Soft Power was based on the three pillars of culture, values and foreign policy. By an accordingly positive perception of these three areas a state A or its way of life will be assessed as attractive by state B. In this case state B will follow voluntarily the approach of state A. Therefore the attraction of these three pillars is vital for the success of Soft Power.

"We must change our mind-set about war itself – to prevent conflict through diplomacy, and strive to end conflicts after they have begun... ."[1] This declaration from President Obama at the Hiroshima Peace Memorial clarifies the importance of international diplomacy as an efficient instrument of Soft Power. Also E. Wilson underlined that good diplomacy can prevent bad military conflicts[2].

"The expected future security environment in 2035 will become more complex than today. In consequence, NATO has to develop new paths and alternative means to increase its capacity to respond flexibly to all kinds and all levels of threats"[3] and "NATO is a military and political alliance"[4]. Against the background of these two assumptions, it is necessary to prove if in future, up to 2035, NATO will be able,

---

[1] Barack Obama, Speech at Hiroshima, 27 May 2016.
[2] Ernest J. Wilson III, "Hard-Power, Soft-Power, Smart Power", 2008, p. 122.
[3] NDC SC130 Ctte#5 MP April 2017, p. 8 paragraph 12.
[4] Joris Ghesquiere, NDC SC130 Q&A session, 12 April 2017.

beside deterrence by Hard Power, to take preventive measures by Soft Power.

The last years have pointed out that NATO has become increasingly fragile. What are the reasons for this fragility? How can NATO reduce this tendency? Are there other means than Hard Power which can be used for crisis prevention or crisis management? Is Soft Power able to conduct this task? Is an institution like NATO able to possess sufficient Soft Power? Among other things these key questions have to be analyzed.

The existing definitions of Soft Power are numerous and this is often the problem regarding a common understanding of the execution of Soft Power. At least it is one means to conduct indirect the power of a state or political actors to achieve their goals. Due to this imprecise description of Soft Power, the next paragraph will illustrate the academic status and will provide a complex definition of Soft Power as basis for further consideration.

You can only deploy Soft Power effectively, if you have enough Hard Power[5]. "A Soft Power solution is not able to displace the need for reliable military options"[6]. "Soft Power is still power, but for NATO primarily Hard Power is needed"[7]. These statements reveal already that Soft Power will always only be a complementary instrument of power. The question is not the renunciation of Hard Power, but its optimal reinforcement by Soft Power. After the identification that NATO in general has Soft Power as an instrument of power, the paper will develop ideas how Soft Power can be integrated profitable in the three NATO core tasks and how Soft Power can support achieving the goals of NATO. Finally, courses of action will be recommended. The three most import remaining and new arising open issues, whose academic and serious answering would blow the extent of this document, will be proposed as necessity for further investigation.

---

[5] Richard Nossal, "Soft power is useless – hard power overwhelms", In: "Journal of Commerce", October 1998.

[6] Stanley R. Sloan, Heiko Borchert, "Soft-Power als Lösung", p. 95.

[7] Robert Johnson, NDC SC130 Q&A session, 10 March 2017.

Soft Power

The original demarcation of Nye that Hard Power is composed of military and economic power and that all other resources belong to Soft Power, was revised by him in 2008[8]. Following his current view there are no more pure Soft Power resources, but all kind of power resources always will serve and improve Soft Power potential. Due to the consistent scientific inaccuracy of Nye (also after his book in 2011)[9] and the high probability of a misinterpretation of his Soft Power definition, this damages the goal that Soft Power finds a bigger use especially in the US political environment. Todd Hall even criticizes Soft Power as a political 'draught', which has only the purpose to strengthen liberal positions towards conservative ones to get monetary funds for Soft Power.[10] This unidirectional perception does not correspond to the state of the science, but underlines the really unilateral perspective of the political elite in the USA.

Based on the latest scientific findings, there is a conceptual difference between the resources, the Soft Power currencies benignity, beauty and brilliance, the instruments to propagate the messages, as well as a direct exercise of influence on decision-makers or indirectly through society and finally between active and passive influencing[11]. Annex A shows and explains the complicated Soft Power mode of operation. This graphical model is an improvement of another model[12] and will serve as the basis for the following research.

NATO and Smart Power

The strong political orientation of NATO, its huge partnership network and solidarity theoretical based on common values in a common culture environment demonstrate one of the strengths of the alliance and therefore it can be followed that NATO should have Soft

---

[8] Joseph S. Nye, "Public Diplomacy and Soft Power", 2008.

[9] Joseph S. Nye, "The Future of Power" 2011.

[10] Todd Hall, "An Unclear Attraction: A Critical Examination of Soft Power as an Analytical Category", 2010.

[11] Joseph S. Nye, "The Future of Power" 2011 , p. 94.

[12] Jan Kersten, "Soft Power und Militär", Potsdam 2012, p. 20.

Power as an independent means of power. The outcomes of this are now the questions, what are the quantitative and qualitative dimensions of this Soft Power potential and how stable and usable is it? Are these resources institutionalized enough to support the tasks or at the moment does Soft Power suffers due to its subordinate position and a lack of resources?

"Hard Power and Soft Power are most effective when they will be used in combination"[13]. On the one hand Stanley R. Sloan and Heiko Borchert leave no doubt that only with a balanced combination of both can policy achieve the optimal effect to reach its goals. On the other hand the well-founded investigation, made by Kersten[14], clearly shows that on the tactical level the rules to execute Soft Power and the necessary logic of military actions often contradict each other. Therefore, it is essential for NATO to develop a strategic and coordinated approach about the positive supplement with Soft Power. This optimal combination of Hard Power and Soft Power is subsumed under the term Smart Power.

Fragility of NATO

"European security has entered a period of intense fragility".[15] Robin Niblett mentions three reasons for this evolution: First of all Russia's increasing offensive infiltration of the European democratic structures which will go on for the next decades, secondly the weakening of the Trans-Atlantic link and thirdly, the massive disagreement between the European governments to respond to external threats. Additionally, there are nationalistic developments in European countries, which all question the established community of values: "I would use the notion of a "Western Community of Values" in the present with great caution"[16][17]. This will be valid also 2035 as long as Europe is

---

[13] Stanley R. Sloan, Heiko Borchert, "Soft-Power als Lösung", p. 81.

[14] Jan Kersten, "Soft Power und Militär", Potsdam 2012, p. 97.

[15] Robin Niblett, "Fragility in Europe is on the rise, and we are not doing enough to respond".

[16] Heinrich August Winkler; Interview with "Stern Magazin", January 2017.

[17] Heinrich August Winkler; Interview with "Stern Magazin", January 2017.

not able to change this development. The British decision to leave the EU is reinforcing European misery.

Europe represents 25 of the 28 NATO member states and therefore an insufficient and poor European coherence has always had a huge impact on the cohesion of NATO. For the military alliance further disturbances are aggravated by the sensitive issue of Burden-Sharing as it was two decades ago and as it will be also in 2035 and the disturbing antidemocratic development in Turkey, which will continue the next years. This is all happening at a time when the global and European security risks for the wider future are becoming more numerous and more complex and at the same time there is a development that the credibility, the performance[18] and the reputation[19] of NATO will decrease.

It is therefore necessary to strengthen the internal cohesion of the Alliance ("An effective, long-term method of creating deep seated solidarity would be to develop a NATO-Culture"[20]) and externally to increase the attractiveness of NATO. These goals can only be achieved as a long-term objective and mainly with the support of national political instruments. But in any case NATO is able to supplementally reinforce this process with its own Soft Power and it should do so. "NATO strategic communications aim…to: c. Contribute to general public awareness and understanding of NATO as part of a broader and on-going public diplomacy effort."[21] With the Centre of Excellence for Strategic Communication in Riga, NATO already has an instrument to execute Soft Power. However, it is necessary, through the capabilities of Public Diplomacy and Public Affairs, to place and to communicate the core messages of a NATO culture, which has to be developed, more actively, more offensively, more emphatically and more sustainably.

---

[18] Knud Bartels, General (ret.), NDC SC130 Q&A session, 04 April 2017.

[19] Ayman Khalil, NDC SC130 Q&A session, 06 April 2017.

[20] Editorial Team, "Enhancing NATO Cohesion: A Framework for 21st Century Solidarity", Paragraph 3.1.

[21] Centre of Excellence for Strategic Communication. Homepage, "About Strategic Communications", Riga.

NATO and Attractiveness

These messages are only credible and only plausible if NATO is sufficiently attractive in the sense of the above-defined model of Soft Power. Benignity, Beauty and Brilliance are the currencies that must be achieved to make NATO more attractive. This makes it possible to generate more Soft Power on its own terms firstly to improve the cohesion of the member states, secondly to prevent crises, and, thirdly, to reinforce the three NATO core tasks as best as possible.

Peter van Hann does not question the effect of Soft Power, but refers to its fragility, due to the fact that the foundation for Soft Power is moral integrity.[22] Following his logic, the currency of Benignity is very vulnerable. If one or more NATO member states make a legally or morally dubious military solo role which is not officially conducted under the NATO mandate, this always invariably falls back on the credibility of the alliance. Benignity can only be generated in the long term by the value-based behaviour of all allies. Beauty is a very subjective currency that from the perspective of external civilian viewers cannot be reconciled at the same time with a military alliance and its lethal products. As a result, this currency can be generated only indirectly and only in a very limited way by the individual member states and then transferred to NATO. Regarding the currency Brilliance the situation is different. Military success, military technical high-performance products, efficient and effective missions with a comprehensive approach, well-respected educational institutions as well as outstanding personalities are elements that NATO as an institution directly and indirectly possesses and which can still be generated with Hard Power and Soft Power.

Stability through Flexibility

The new complex challenges for NATO, mentioned above, always require an appropriate response. The more flexible NATO is in facing the current and upcoming threats, the more successful the alliance will be. Taking previously mentioned restrictions into consideration, NATO is able to enhance its flexibility by increasing the number of

---

[22] Peter van Hann, "Power Public Diplomacy and the Pax Americana", New York 2005.

courses of action, through the execution of its existing potential of Soft Power.

However, the application of Soft Power by NATO does not mean that NATO will become 'softer', but it will become 'smarter' and more successful, based on its Hard Power and Soft Power. "Most important, in today's age of globalization, information revolution and broadened participation, citizens in democracies must learn more about the nature and limits of our all-too-human leadership"[23]. It is now urgently necessary that the political leaders on both sides of the Atlantic learn and implement two things. Firstly, NATO needs both, Hard- and Soft Power, to become more stable and successful, and secondly, societies, especially the European ones, need to be informed of the necessity of military means in a more comprehensive way in order to get their long-term consensus and support.

Conclusion and Proposals

From a scientific point of view Soft Power as a Power-Concept is too new in order to have sufficiently robust research-results on the application and limits of this instrument of power. At the same time, however, Soft Power is unquestionably a complex, highly effective and, in contrast to Hard Power, a cost-effective means of achieving objectives through attractiveness. Therefore, there is need for more comprehensive scientific investigations that would go far beyond the scope of this document on the subject of Soft Power in general and Soft Power and NATO in particular. How can Soft Power be optimally complemented with Hard Power? How can NATO itself generate Soft Power and how can NATO benefit best from the Soft Power of its Member States? Which means are available within NATO to implement Soft Power and which kind of new and additional instruments have to be institutionalized?

Soft Power as a concept of power works only if the goods of the owner are attractive. NATO has been attractive over the past two decades in that sense that it could increase its membership by 12 states. However, the reasons were based primarily on the need for

---

[23] Joseph S. Ney, "The Powers to Lead" 2011, p. 145.

security and protection that NATO promises to offer to its Member States. In any case, NATO's Soft Power cannot be used directly as a deterrent, but it can have an indirect effect for NATO's three core tasks as follows. Soft Power can be used firstly to increase the credibility and cohesion of the alliance to serve the Collective Defence, secondly to support crisis management through a common value-based and standardized training and, finally, to strengthen the international networking and the establishment of educational institutions to improve cooperative security. Due to its sensitivity to external disturbances, Soft Power is generally very fragile as an instrument of power; especially for an institution of 28 countries like NATO with 28 different political interests. This limits its impacts. Since values are not universal[24], the use of Soft Power across cultural borders[25] in the short and medium term is only conditionally promising.

In the area of conflict prevention the consistent use of Soft Power by NATO can achieve complementary and positive results. For its practical implementation four main measures are recommended. Firstly, to develop a more active information policy via its own radio and television stations as well as Internet portals, in which globally relevant security and economic policy events will be assessed comprehensively together with background information. Secondly, using again the instrument media create and publicise a long-term NATO image change across cultural boundaries in order to produce attractiveness by showing flexibility, reliability, success, capacity to act, enforcement, value orientation and multilateralism. Thirdly the enlargement of existing training capacities (for example, the Joint Force Training Centre (JFTC) in Bydgoszcz) and the implementation of a value-oriented, jointly prepared training of soldiers from all nations which will participate in NATO operations. Fourth, and most recently, the foundation and establishment of open NATO universities in areas such as politics, history, economics, linguistics, information technology and engineering to educate and train academically personnel from national

---

[24] Christopher Coker, "Does a Transatlantic Strategy Exist?", Video Brussels Jan 2015, 27:25min.

[25] Renato Cruz de Castro, "Confronting China's Charm Offensive in East Asia: A Simple Case of Fighting Fire with Fire?", 2009, p. 77.

foreign, domestic, economic or development aid ministries, as well as officers from NATO countries, NATO partner countries and other states of other cultures with which bilateral agreements have been concluded.

"Smart Power is a meaningful concept and NATO can certainly use it, but ultimately the share of Soft Power has to be coordinated with various organizations such as the EU, in order to achieve a higher degree of effectiveness and to avoid redundancies."[26] This statement summarizes NATO's possibilities but also its limitations regarding Smart Power. But in any case there is no doubt that Smart Power can and will increase the flexibility of NATO.

---

[26] Denis Mercier, General, NDC SC130 FS2 Visit ACT Q&A session, 08 May 2017.

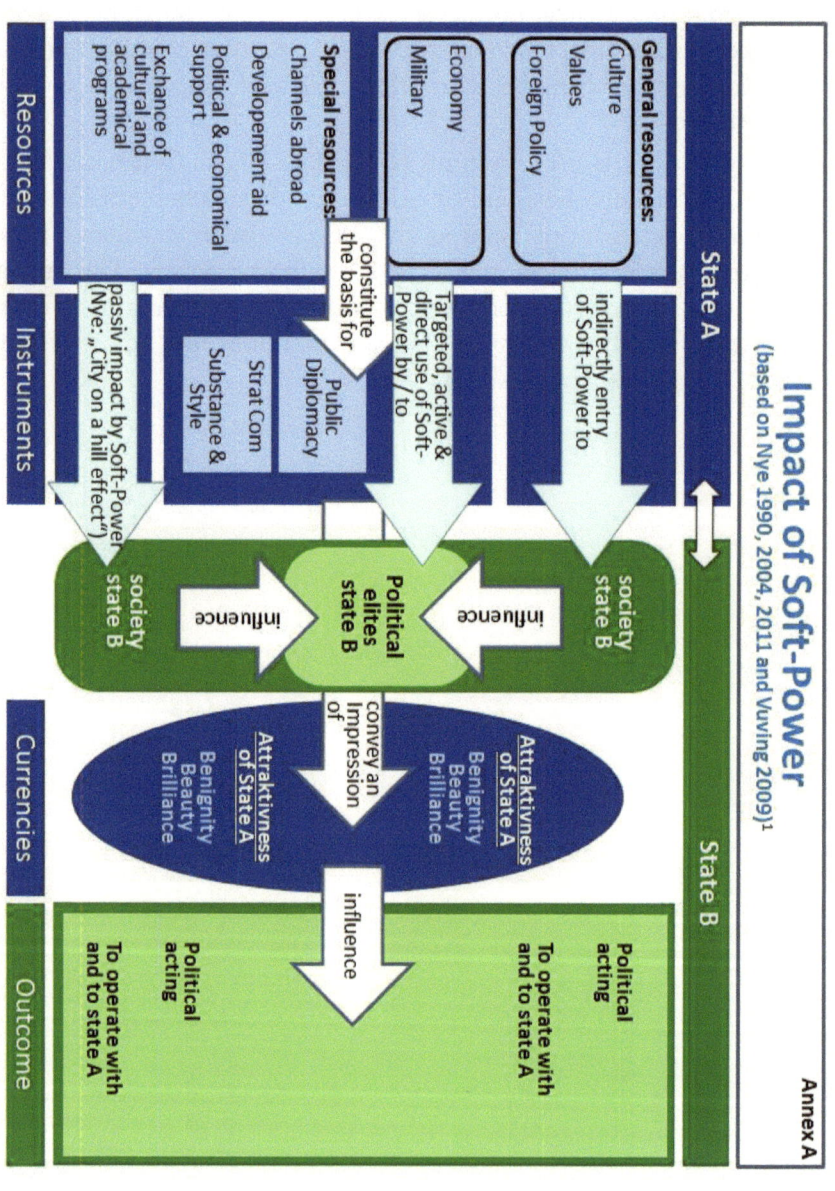

Bibliography

Adnan, Indra. "Soft Power: Britain is losing its grip on this key asset", In: "The Guardian", March 31st 2014.

Bartels, Knud, General (ret). "NATO in the Post-Cold War Order: Challenges and Implications", NDC SC130 Q&A session, Rome, April 04th 2017.

Berenskötter, Felix, M.J. Williams. "Power in World Politics". New York 2007.

Bilgin Pinar, Berivan Elis. "Hard Power, Soft Power: Toward a More Realistic Power Analysis". In: "Insight Turkey Vol.10, No.2, 2008", Ankara, page 5-20.

Center for Strategic Research. "The Role of Diplomacy and Soft Power in Combatting Terrorism". Ankara May 29th 2014.

Centre of Excellence for Strategic Communication, Homepage, "About Strategic Communications", Riga.

Coker, Christopher. "Does a Transatlantic Strategy Exist?". Video Brussels Jan 2015, 27:25min.

Cruz de Castro, Renato. "Confronting China´s Charm Offensive in East Asia: A Simple Case of Fighting Fire with Fire?", In: *"Issues & Studies. 45(1)"* 2009, page 77.

Deutscher Bundestag – Wissenschaftliche Dienste Nr.45/06 – Soft Power, Berlin, November 03rd 2006.

Editorial Team, "Enhancing NATO Cohesion: A Framework for 21st Century Solidarity", In: *"Atlantic-Cummunity.Org – The Open Think Tank on Foreign Policy"*, August 2016.

Gallarotti, Guilio M. "Smart Power: Definitions, Importance and Effectiveness". In: *"The Journal of Strategic Studies, 2015, Vol.38, No.3"*. Connecticut 2015.

Ghesquiere, Joris. "NATO Resource Policy", NDC SC130 Q&A session, Rome, April, 12th 2017.

Hall, Todd. "An Unclear Attraction: A Critical Examination of Soft Power as an Analytical Category", In: *"The Chinese Journal of International Politics 3"*, 2010, page 189-211.

van Hann, Peter. "Power Public Diplomacy and the Pax Americana", In: *"The New Public Diplomacy. Soft Power in International Relations"*, New York 2005.

Johnson, Robert. "Conflict and Confrontation: The Changing Nature of Conflict", Rome, NDC SC130 Q&A session, March 10th 2017.

Kagan, Robert. "Of Paradise and Power: America and Europe in the New World Order", New York 2003.

Khalil, Ayman. "NATO´s Partnership Initiatives", NDC SC130 Q&A session, Rome, 06. April 06th 2017.

Kersten, Jan. "Soft Power und Militär", Potsdam 2012.

Lee, Donna, Paul Sharp. "The New Public Diplomacy – Soft Power in International Relations". New York 2005.

Mercier, Denis, General, NDC SC130 FS2 Visit ACT Q&A session, Norfolk, May 08th 2017.

NDC SC130 Ctte#5 MP April 2017, page 8 paragraph 12.

Niblett, Robin. "Fragility in Europe is on the rise, and we are not doing enough to respond", In: *"World Economic Forum Annual Meeting 2017"*,

https://www.weforum.org/agenda/2017/01/fragility-in-europe-is-on-the-rise-and-we-re-not-doing-enough-to-respond/

Nossal, Richard. "Soft power is useless – hard power overwhelms", In: *"Journal of Commerce"*, October 1998.

Nye, Joseph S. "Bound To Lead: The Changing Nature of American Power", New York 1990.

Nye, Joseph S. "Soft Power. The Means to Success in World Politics", New York 2004.

Nye, Joseph S. "The Powers to Lead", New York 2008.

Nye, Joseph S. "Public Diplomacy and Soft Power". In: *"The ANNALS of the American Academy of Political and Social Science. 616 (1)"*, 2008, page 94-109.

Nye, Joseph S. "The Future of Power", 2011.

Nye, Joseph S. "Die USA haben Soft Power eingebüßt", DW-Interview with Michael Knigge, January 16th 2017

Obama, Barack. Speech at the Hiroshima Peace Memorial, May 27th 2016.

Sloan, Stanley R., Heiko Borchert, "Soft-Power als Lösung", In: "*OSCE-Annual 2003*", page 81-95.

Szumowski, Adrian. "The Idea of Smart Power in the Concept of NATO security". In: "*NATO – Towards the Challenges of a Contemporary World*", Warsaw 2013, page 227-246

Vuving, Alexander L. "How Soft Power Works". Presented at the panel "*Soft Power and Smart Power*", American Political Science Association annual meeting, Toronto, September 3rd, 2009.

Walker, Christopher. "The Hijacking of Soft Power". In: "*Journal of Democracy*", Washington, January 2016.

Wilson, Jeanne L. "Soft Power: A Comparison of Discourse and Practice in Russia and China". In: "*Europe-Asia Studies – Vol.67, No.8*". October 2015, page 1171-1202.

Wilson III, Ernest J. "Hard Power, Soft Power, Smart Power", In: "*The ANNALS of the American Academy of Political and Social Science 2008 616*", 2008, page 110-124.

Winkler, Heinrich August. Interview with "Stern Magazin", January 2017,
https://www.google.it/search?client=safari&channel=ipad_bm&ei=iOEaWbi5F4nDgAaa_5O4CA&q=heinrich+august+winkler+interview+stern+2017&oq=heinrich+august+winkler+interview+stern+2017&gs_l=mobile-gws-serp.3...97656.110381.0.111560.9.9.0.0.0.0.180.855.5j4.9.0....0...1.1.64.mobile-gws-serp..0.8.757...0i22i30k1j33i160k1j33i21k1.RcF8cYTHeiQ

The Authors

All authors took part in the Senior Course 130 at the NATO Defense College in Rome from February till July 2017. The views expressed here are the authors' and do not necessarily reflect the official position of the Government of Germany and of The Netherlands or any of their departments or agencies.

Jan Ballast, M.A., is a senior staff member, involved with foreign intelligence, mission support and national security, working for the Ministry of Defence of The Netherlands.

Willi Bentzinger, M.Sc., is a civil servant in the armament branch of the German Ministry of Defence. His current position is division leader in the Bundeswehr Technical Center for Aircraft and Aeronautical Equipment in Manching.

Uwe Hartmann, Ph.D., M.A., is Colonel (GS) in the German Army. He is a Visiting Lecturer/Military Professor at the Naval Postgraduate School in Monterey/CA.

Caroline Linzenmeier is a lawyer. She works as a desk officer (civ) in the German Ministry of Defence in Berlin.

Jörg Modey, M.A., is Captain (Navy) in the German Navy. He is Dean and Deputy Commander at the Naval Academy in Flensburg Mürwick.

Lutz Mühlhöfer is Colonel in the German Air Force. He is Deputy Commander and Chief of Staff of the German Air Force Officer School in Fürstenfeldbruck.

Frank Wasgindt, M.A., is Colonel (GS) in the German Army. He is the Director International Advanced Command and Staff Course at the Führungsakademie der Bundeswehr in Hamburg.

Carola Hartmann Miles-Verlag

Politik, Gesellschaft, Militär

Uwe Hartmann, *Innere Führung. Erfolge und Defizite der Führungsphilosophie für die Bundeswehr,* Berlin 2007.

Hans-Christian Beck, Christian Singer (Hrsg.), *Entscheiden – Führen – Verantworten. Soldatsein im 21. Jahrhundert,* Berlin 2011.

Reiner Pommerin (ed.), *Clausewitz goes global. Carl von Clausewitz in the 21st Century,* Berlin 2011.

Eberhard Birk, Winfried Heinemann, Sven Lange (Hrsg.), *Tradition für die Bundeswehr. Neue Aspekte einer alten Debatte,* Berlin 2012.

Holger Müller, *Clausewitz' Verständnis von Strategie im Spiegel der Spieltheorie,* Berlin 2012.

Angelika Dörfler-Dierken, *Führung in der Bundeswehr,* Berlin 2013.

Cornelia Fedtke, Kai-Uwe Hellmann, Jan Hörmann, *Migration und Militär. Zur Integration deutscher Soldaten mit Migrationshintergrund in der Bundeswehr,* Berlin 2013.

Torsten Konopka, *Afrikanische Wehrsysteme und ihre Entwicklung zwischen 1990/91 und 2011,* Berlin 2014.

Wolf Graf von Baudissin, *Grundwert Frieden in Politik – Strategie – Führung von Streitkräften,* hrsg. von Claus von Rosen, Berlin 2014.

Wolf Graf von Baudissin, *Der Widerstand. „... um nie wieder in die auswegslose Lage zu geraten...",* hrsg. von Claus von Rosen, Berlin 2014.

Marcel Bohnert, Lukas J. Reitstetter (Hrsg.), *Armee im Aufbruch. Zur Gedankenwelt junger Offiziere in den Kampftruppen der Bundeswehr,* Berlin 2014.

Arjan Kozica, Kai Prüter, Hannes Wendroth (Hrsg.), *Unternehmen Bundeswehr? Theorie und Praxis (militärischer) Führung,* Berlin 2014.

Angelika Dörfler-Dierken, Robert Kramer, *Innere Führung in Zahlen. Streitkräftebefragung 2013,* Berlin 2014.

Phil C. Langer, Gerhard Kümmel (Hrsg.), *„Wir sind Bundeswehr." Wie viel Vielfalt benötigen/vertragen die Streitkräfte?,* Berlin 2015.

Dirk Freudenberg, *Counterinsurgency. Aufstandsbekämpfung als Phase zur Überwindung schwacher Staatlichkeit und zur Etablierung des Aufbaus einer stabilen Nachkriegsordnung?,* Berlin 2016.

Alois Bach, Walter Sauer (Hrsg.), *Schützen.Retten.Kämpfen. Dienen für Deutschland*, Berlin 2016.

Dirk Freudenberg, Stephan Maninger, *Neue Kriege. Sicherheitspolitische Rahmenbedingungen, Mentalitäten, Strategien, Methoden und Instrumente*, Berlin 2016.

Claas Siano, *Die Luftwaffe und der Starfighter*, Berlin 2016.

Eberhard Birk, Peter Andreas Popp, *Luftwaffenoffizier 21. Das Selbstverständnis des Luftwaffenoffiziers zu Beginn des 21. Jahrhunderts*, Berlin 2016.

Eberhard Birk, Heiner Möllers (Hrsg.), *Luftwaffe und Luftverteidigung*, Berlin 2017.

Alessandro Rappazzo, *Vorsprung durch Leadership. Modernes Leadership in der Armee*, Berlin 2017.

Oliver Schmidt, *Deutsche Außenpolitik und die Zukunft der nuklearen Teilhabe in der NATO*, Berlin 2017.

Wolfgang Peischel (Hrsg.), *Wiener Strategie-Konferenz 2016. Strategie neu denken*, Berlin 2017.

Dirk Freudenberg, *Theorie des Irregulären – Erscheinungen und Abgrenzungen von Partisanen, Guerillas und Terroristen im Modernen Kleinkrieg sowie Entwicklungstendenzen der Reaktion*, Bd. 1-3, Berlin 2017.

Donald Abenheim and Carolyn Halladay, *Soldiers, War, Knowledge and Citizenship: German-American Essays on Civil-Military Relations*, Berlin 2017.

Jahrbuch Innere Führung

Uwe Hartmann, Claus von Rosen, Christian Walther (Hrsg.), *Jahrbuch Innere Führung 2009. Die Rückkehr des Soldatischen*, Eschede 2009.

Helmut R. Hammerich, Uwe Hartmann, Claus von Rosen (Hrsg.), *Jahrbuch Innere Führung 2010. Die Grenzen des Militärischen*, Berlin 2010.

Uwe Hartmann, Claus von Rosen, Christian Walther (Hrsg.), *Jahrbuch Innere Führung 2011. Ethik als geistige Rüstung für Soldaten*, Berlin 2011.

Uwe Hartmann, Claus von Rosen, Christian Walther (Hrsg.), *Jahrbuch Innere Führung 2012. Der Soldatenberuf zwischen gesellschaftlicher Integration und suis generis-Ansprüchen,* Berlin 2012.

Uwe Hartmann, Claus von Rosen (Hrsg.), *Jahrbuch Innere Führung 2013. Wissenschaften und ihre Relevanz für die Bundeswehr als Armee im Einsatz,* Berlin 2013.

Uwe Hartmann, Claus von Rosen (Hrsg.), *Jahrbuch Innere Führung 2014. Drohnen, Roboter und Cyborgs – Der Soldat im Angesicht neuer Militärtechnologien,* Berlin 2014.

Uwe Hartmann, Claus von Rosen (Hrsg.), *Jahrbuch Innere Führung 2015. Neue Denkwege angesichts der Gleichzeitigkeit unterschiedlicher Krisen, Konflikte und Kriege,* Berlin 2015.

Uwe Hartmann, Claus von Rosen (Hrsg.), *Jahrbuch Innere Führung 2016. Innere Führung als kritische Instanz,* Berlin 2016.

Einsatzerfahrungen

Kay Kuhlen, *Um des lieben Friedens willen. Als Peacekeeper im Kosovo,* Eschede 2009.

Sascha Brinkmann, Joachim Hoppe (Hrsg.), *Generation Einsatz, Fallschirmjäger berichten ihre Erfahrungen aus Afghanistan,* Berlin 2010.

Artur Schwitalla, *Afghanistan, jetzt weiß ich erst… Gedanken aus meiner Zeit als Kommandeur des Provincial Reconstruction Team FEYZABAD,* Berlin 2010.

Uwe Hartmann, *War without Fighting? The Reintegration of Former Combatants in Afghanistan seen through the Lens of Strategic Thought,* Berlin 2014.

Rainer Buske, *KUNDUZ. Ein Erlebnisbericht über einen militärischen Einsatz der Bundeswehr in AFGHANISTAN im Jahre 2008,* Berlin ^{2}2016.

Monterey Studies

Uwe Hartmann, *Carl von Clausewitz and the Making of Modern Strategy,* Potsdam 2002.

Zeljko Cepanec, *Croatia and NATO. The Stony Road to Membership,* Potsdam 2002.

Ekkehard Stemmer, *Demography and European Armed Forces,* Berlin 2006.

Sven Lange, *Revolt against the West. A Comparison of the Current War on Terror with the Boxer Rebellion in 1900-01,* Berlin 2007.

Klaus M. Brust, *Culture and the Transformation of the Bundeswehr,* Berlin 2007.

Donald Abenheim, *Soldier and Politics Transformed,* Berlin 2007.

Michael Stolzke, *The Conflict Aftermath. A Chance for Democracy: Norm Diffusion in Post-Conflict Peace Building,* Berlin 2007.

Frank Reimers, *Security Culture in Times of War. How did the Balkan War affect the Security Cultures in Germany and the United States?,* Berlin 2007.

Michael G. Lux, *Innere Führung – A Superior Concept of Leadership?,* Berlin 2009.

Marc A. Walther, *HAMAS between Violence and Pragmatism,* Berlin 2010.

Frank Hagemann, *Strategy Making in the European Union,* Berlin 2010.

Ralf Hammerstein, *Deliberalization in Jordan: the Roles of Islamists and U.S.-EU Assistance in stalled Democratization,* Berlin 2011.

Jochen Wittmann, *Auftragstaktik,* Berlin 2012.

Michael Hanisch, *On German Foreign und Security Policy. Determinants of German Military Engagement in Africa since 2011,* Berlin 2015.

Gregoire Monnet, *The Evolution of Strategic Thought since September 11, 2001,* Berlin 2016.

Stefan Klein, *America First? – Isolationism in U.S. Foreign Policy from the 19th to the 21st Century,* Berlin 2017.

www.miles-verlag.jimdo.com